THE INHERITANCE

A Stock-Picking Story

PAMELA AYO YETUNDE

MARABELLA BOOKS
Oakland, California

Marabella Books
4096 Piedmont Avenue PMB 307
Oakland, California 94611
510.337.3262
http://www.smartsisters.com

Book design by Tracey Scott
Cover art and design by Randolph Belle
Author photograph © 1999, Jim Dennis. Used with permission.

ISBN 1-928775-04-7
Library of Congress Card Number: 00-107366

We would like to hear from you. If you have comments or suggestions or you would like to order additional copies of this book, please write or call us at: Marabella Books, 4096 Piedmont Avenue, PMB 307, Oakland, CA 94611; 510-337-3262; www.smartsisters.com

Dedicated to the memories of
Curtis W. Pinner,
Sylvia Ann Martin, and
Clara Arbella Bailey Norwood

Table of Contents

Introduction

This book was written for the descendants of the slave and working classes, and those of you in the U.S. who are here to improve your economic condition, but may be doing so under less than ideal working conditions. It is written for the descendants of American Indians killed in the struggle for the preservation of their nations, and for the descendants of the Chinese whose laundry businesses were disrupted. It is for the descendants of the Japanese who were "interned" and the descendants of Africans who have not received an apology or reparations.

Why a book on investing for "the rest of us?" Part of our collective legacies may be an antipathy for the "new nation" that our ancestors passed down from generation to generation. You may wonder if being a black, brown, yellow or red U.S. citizen means you can pursue economic liberty and monetary happiness. The answer is a resounding, "yes." You may be thinking, "but I'm not a descendant of the working classes or "I have no antipathy toward the U.S. Is this book for me?" It is if you want to learn about investing in the stock market.

Today, the buying and selling of stocks takes place without racial discrimination and the need for remedial action. As a matter of fact, it is probably the one place you can build wealth without regard to your appearance or belief system. The stock market is the "leveler" in a world in which a person with a G.E.D. can build as much or more wealth than someone with a medical or law degree.

The story centers around an African-American family and their African-American stock broker. The Jamisons come into an inheritance of stock and their broker, B.B. Freeman, attempts to help them learn how to invest.

Many people in the African-American community argue that the reason why we do not know as much as we should about the stock market is because our foreparents did not invest. Others argue that we have not resolved the political, religious, historical and economic issues around what it means to invest in an economic system that is still deemed by some as exploitative of people of color and poor people. Through this fictional story you will learn about the issues and how to overcome them through the instructional lessons and advice on how to invest in the stock market.

The characters and story are fictional but inspired by real events and companies. The magazine and newspaper stories are fictional. Real-world financial lessons and definitions are interspersed throughout in order to put the stories in context.

I hope that this book will be shared with family members throughout the next generation. To that end, the book is not composed of only topical information but is full of fundamental information and advice that is not subject to change anytime soon.

It only takes a few hours to read the book, but it takes several months to several years to become a good investor. Please keep in mind as you read the book – it becomes more complex the deeper you go. If you've wondered what makes stocks go up and down in price, there's no ignoring the charts. The more you read them, the more you'll understand them.

Overall, I hope you enjoy this story. If you've never invested, or if you're a beginning investor, you'll be able to apply the information easily. If you're an experienced investor, this book should bring some clarity to what you're already doing. Thank you for allowing me the opportunity to share these thoughts with you. I hope this book helps you secure your financial future and the future of generations to come.

Thank You

One of the greatest joys I have in life is being surrounded by intelligent and thoughtful people who are willing to take time away from the things they really want to do to help me in what I really want to do. I want to thank my clients and those who have attended my seminars. These people have asked me questions and provided insight into how I can better share investment information.

I am eternally grateful to Tracey L. Scott for editing and publishing my books.

I also want to thank my colleagues Jane Davey and Cathy Kosley for providing their feedback from a financial professional's perspective. Maria DeMarco, Gail Spann, Deloris Scott and Betsy Warren also provided constructive feedback, making the book more "readable." I had a lot of fun and received a lot of great feedback from the CACTUS Investment Group (Cynthia Bagby, Sharon McGaffie, Cydne Nash, Elson Nash, and Judy Ward), Reggie Harris, Dara Efron, Dorothea Crosbie-Taylor and Jan Crosbie-Taylor. Thank you all for the laughs and the friendly banter.

Elder William Z. Scott provided religious insight. Felicia Poe and Paul Robertson helped me with the research. The book would not have been written without them. Lastly, I'd like to acknowledge Perris McKnight, Barbara Stanny, and The Everywoman's Money Conference co-founders Jan Black and Jody Temple-White for opening their network to me.

Pamela Ayo Yetunde
July, 2000
Oakland, California

Prologue

Some buildings serve only as structures; other buildings stand as monuments. With one touch of the solid brass doorknob and one push of the four-inch thick mahogany door leading into the inner sanctum, you knew you were inside a monument. Looking across the room, you knew you must take a journey through time, each visit being a Mecca of sorts, before getting to the desk. Before setting foot on that journey, you stood in awe of the round, ebony-paneled office with the stamped tin ceiling. Then you began to remember all that had been said about the place. The office, known as one of the most beautifully designed offices occupied by a Black man, had been featured in architectural and gossip magazines alike. You felt like you had walked into a king's domain, and, depending on your allegiances, you had.

The stained glass window featuring a Black Jesus surrounded by Black Disciples and Black angels demonstrated the most exquisite modern-day craftsmanship. In contrast to this opulence, the scattered furniture provided only enough seating for four people in a room that could have easily accommodated twenty-five.

It was all quite intimidating, so much so that the path to the desk followed a certain routine and ceremony. Tightly woven Persian rugs created a concentric pattern that you walked between, almost like a maze, leading to the desk. The rugs looked fresh from the desert, as if no one had walked on them – and they had not.

Six life-sized oil portraits of the ministers of Mt. Zion A.M.E. Church graced the outer walls. The seven bookshelves, one dedicated to each minister, reached as high as the ceilings, and separated each portrait, one from the other. The first book on each shelf was a version of the Bible, followed by the next favorite book of that particular pastor. There were many books – W.E.B. DuBois, Martin Luther King, Jr., The Autobiography of Malcolm X – and more recent writings by Cornel West and Henry Louis Gates, Jr. Mostly though, the shelves contained obscure religious writings that surely only theology students would have read.

Only after circling the office could you approach the seating area in front of the desk. The well-worn couch matched the chair with deep brown leather and brass tacks. Story has it that the furniture originally belonged to the founding pastor, who received his calling while sitting on the couch.

If you were ever invited to take a seat, you came face-to-face with the pastor, and effectively with all the pastors before him represented in oil. This was where you met the fiery robed man on the pulpit, and thus, this is where you found your spiritual self. Yes, it was all *quite* intimidating.

Pastor number seven, the Reverend Marcus Jamison, walked the dizzying circle to his desk, sat down, and began casually reading the front page of his newspaper. But this time, something caused an emotional reaction:

> ***Houston Chronicle***, October 31 - ACBN, the ticker symbol for Ashanti Cable Broadcasting Network (ACB) Holdings, began trading on the New York Stock Exchange (NYSE). ACBN is the first Black-owned company to trade on the NYSE. Trading started at $17 per share and closed that day at $23 1/2 per share. 4.25 million shares representing 21% ownership in the company were offered to the public for sale. Donald Jackson, founder, chair, CEO and president, owns 56% of the shares. 400,000 shares were sold to individuals. The lead underwriter is First Maine Corporation.

Reverend Jamison picked up his phone book, frantically flipped the pages, and dialed thinking, "I don't know why I'm still using this rotary phone." He knew why when he noticed the bronze plate with the inscription, "In Dedication to Our Beloved Pastor. The Youth Group, 1973." Yes, this place was a monument.

Underwriter: an investment banker or group of investment bankers who agree to purchase a new issue of stock from the issuing company and distribute it to investors.

"B.B., this is Reverend Jamison, how are you? Look, I've given a lot of thought to what you've been telling me these last few years, and I think I'm ready to take that step. I thought you'd be pleased! I have about $100,000, but please don't tell anyone. I want this kept between me and you.... Well brother, I was just reading about ACB offering some stock to the public, and I think I want to, no, I *know* I want you to take this money and invest it all in ACB. Okay then…just place the order first thing tomorrow at whatever price it's at. Just use the cash in my account. No, no…I'm not backing out of this one…. No, I don't have any other investments, except my house…. No, this is the only company I want to invest in right now….Yes, yes, I know it's risky to invest all of my money in one company, but I think I can handle the risk…. No, I don't think I'll be investing any more any time soon. Just buy me whatever $100,000 will buy me as soon as the market opens tomorrow….Good! I wish I had done this yesterday. Why didn't you let me know about this yesterday!?... I see. Call me later and let me know how many shares I have. Oh, and B.B., I do appreciate your help. Really, I do." He hung up the phone and smiled.

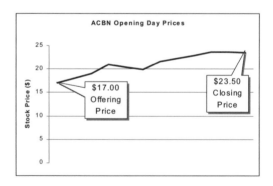

The Street Reports, October 31 – ACB Holdings, Inc.'s public stock offering, its first, was a hit. The 4.25 million-share offering, 21% of the 11-year-old company, was the Big Board's fourth most active issue. Its under-writers – First Maine Corporation – initially priced the shares at $11 to $13 each, based on price-to-earnings ratios of other cable-TV stocks. The shares began trading under the ticker symbol ACBN at $17 each and closed at $23½. That gives ACB Holdings a market value of about $475 million..... CEO Donald Jackson sold only 375,000 shares in Wednesday's offering.... ACB's net income has tripled in the past three years to $9.3 million for the fiscal year that ended July 31. During that time, revenue grew to $50.8 million from $22.5 million. Most of ACB's revenue – 59% in fiscal 1991.... Of the 4.5 million shares made available to the public, African-Americans purchased 227,000 shares (just over 5%), and institutional investors purchased 4,250,000 shares.

The Atlanta Chronicle, November 2 – Donald Jackson earned $6.4 million when he sold 375,000 of his own ACBN shares at $17 each. ACB Holdings sold 1.5 millions shares, raising about $25 million (before expenses) in which one-half would be used to reduce the company's debt. The remainder would go toward improvements in the company's operations.

In the Beginning

The greatest gift lies not in the existence of money but the manifestations of love.

The Funeral: Ishmael's Regrets

As usual, it was sweltering inside. People seemed to come out of the woodwork and linoleum and leather that made up the sanctuary to view, for one last time, the expression on Dad's face. Folks always said he had an interesting face. I didn't know if they found him attractive, ugly or simply interesting. Nevertheless, there they all were, filing behind one another to view his interesting face as his stiff body faced toward heaven, waiting to receive his key to the Pearly Gates.

"Ishmael, Sister Jamison, we were so sorry to hear about Reverend Jamison. He was a good man."

"Sister Jamison, sons, your father was a good preacher, yes sir, he sho' could work up a sermon."

"Boys, Mrs. Jamison, my wife and I are going to miss Reverend Jamison. He was a good man."

The people kept coming, expressing their grief and condolences — one after another, talking about how good Dad was at ministering, how good he was at counseling, how interesting he was. There must have been thousands of people there that day, and we must have said "thank you" several thousand times before the day was over.

We sat there in the first row and listened to another pastor describe Dad's life, as if he knew Dad better than we did. Certainly, he had only noble things to say about Dad, but if I had had the strength, I could have said a whole lot more that would have meant a lot more to my mother, who surely would miss him the most. Crying in public really wasn't an option, so I sat next to Mom and wept silently. The people kept coming, and soon, I didn't recognize any of them. Everyone was shocked by the suddenness of his death. It was as if Houston stood still when the news hit the papers. Yet, three days later, there we were at his funeral. That's what an organized church will do for you.

The man was fit! He didn't smoke, didn't dare drink or do drugs, no history of heart disease in the family, no nothing. No warning whatsoever. He was just gone at age forty-seven. His jogging buddies found him at his desk, slumped over his newspaper, with his telephone book open. The doctors said he had had a heart attack, plain and simple. I don't think Dad thought he was on his way out, not with all the plans he had.

"Son, we're sorry."

"What!?...I mean, thank you." I was annoyed at having no time to think about Dad without constant interruptions by his admirers. By the fourth hour of the funeral, the best we could do was bow our heads in sorrow, look up into their faces, say "thank you" and bow our heads again as if to signal that they should move on and make room for hundreds of others who felt compelled to say something to us.

We all loved Dad very much. The day he died was the worst day of my life. I asked myself: what was life going to be like without Dad? He was always there for me — well, after he was done ministering to his congregation. When he had time, he'd tell me about the Lord, about being Black, about being a Black man, about dating, about careers. He'd take me and Isaac to a football game here and there, but more than anything, he would tell us "If you don't believe in something, you'll fall for anything." That must be true, for as much as Dad stood for Jesus, he fell for nothing. As a matter of fact, he believed in nothing else but the Lord and as a consequence, he believed God would provide everything, as long as he served Jesus. The arguments we'd have about religion and politics. I believed in God but argued for political involvement as the only way to solve social problems. Dad always said that politics would compromise my religious beliefs. I should have told Dad that I loved him and should have told him more than once or twice.

The Funeral: Isaac's Fears

I wasn't worried about Ishmael, but Mom, she was stoic. Since the news, she was very business-like as the women of the church helped her arrange the funeral. I've gone to movies with Mom and watched her cry at the sappiest stuff, but today of all days — nothing. I whispered to her throughout the entire funeral that it would be good to cry now, while surrounded by her family and friends, rather than waiting until she's alone. She responded that she was okay and that if I wanted to cry, that would be all right, that she was there to comfort me and Ishmael, and that nothing would ever change about that.

Her lack of emotion scared me because I thought that maybe she didn't fully understand what had happened. Her husband was dead. They had been married twenty-two years, and Mom relied on him for practically everything. He was her "guiding light," and she was his "shining star." Together, they illuminated every room they entered. They were truly in love. Dad never gave her a reason to question his actions. After he finished seminary, he preached every Sunday; he administered church affairs Tuesday through Friday; he'd take us to a game here or there; and he was home every night. As far as I know, Mom and Dad never spent a night apart.

"Yes, he was a good, good man," I replied as one of the church members took my limp left hand. My right hand gripped Ishmael's shoulder as we sat on either side of Mom, trying to comfort each other and Mom, too. We had to be strong for her, though she had always been the strongest one in the family. The intense pressure of losing the only real man you ever knew made me feel like a boy, helpless. At the age of twenty, Ishmael and I were going to have to step up to the plate, as they say, and be men for Mom. With one year left until graduation from two different colleges, we didn't even have our own money to help out.

I clenched Ishmael's shoulder, leaned toward my mother and turned my head toward Ishmael to get his attention. "Everything will be fine, right, Ishmael? Mom, Ishmael, everything will be fine."

We joined hands, and I cried publicly. I wailed because for the first time, I truly felt fear. Dad's death was like losing a compass in the wilderness. We had no direction.

When Is Too Much Not Enough?

It took some time for the family to get themselves together enough to talk about their father's personal business affairs, but they needed to, especially for their mother's sake. With a greater show of strength than her sons, Julene called the meeting.

As Isaac drove in from school, panic struck. For the first time he thought that his father may have excluded him from his will.

"We never had knock down, drag out fights before, but after his conversion, he never really approved of my world view. Like a dutiful son, I went to church every Sunday until I left for college at eighteen, I didn't get anybody pregnant, I was in college and I was a good athlete. I would have made most fathers proud, but Dad detested the fact that I think money is what makes the world go around. Heck, it was certainly not Jesus (though the world would be a better place for it), but given the choice between money and Jesus, it seemed to me that the most powerful people in the world owned businesses, and bowed to the ol' mighty dollar. Yeah, that's what made the world go 'round, the Church of General Electric, not the Church of Latter-Day Saints."

Isaac took a break from daydreaming to check his gas meter, finding that it was nearly on empty. Setting his mind on getting gas soon, he began to wonder about his own financial situation.

"I sure hope Dad didn't leave me out. He always liked Ishmael best (when he could tell us apart) because Ishmael always had been a do-gooder. Good Ishmael — always helping the needy and saving the world. I told Ishmael that if he wanted to save the world, he should start by saving himself first because a Brother has got to get paid!

"Dad hated when I challenged Ishmael on these matters, but even Dad, underneath all his ministerial garb, secretly agreed with me. He was about the money, for sure, because before he was Reverend Jamison, he was Mr. Marcus Jamison, Manager of the Human Resources Department at Doran, Inc. I remember seeing Dad in his suit and tie every morning and thinking 'that's one bad, successful brother and I'm going to be just like him when I grow up.' Ishmael would say that there was more to Dad than met most people's eyes and that Dad wasn't happy or 'fulfilled.' Unfulfilled? Heck, Dad made more money than most Black men in all of Texas. Yet, Dad would often come home, kiss Mom, say hi to us and follow with, 'Isaac, Ishmael, don't ever work for someone else *after* you've gotten all you can get from them.' He was so angry and so sure that corporations, not the government, were the greatest barriers to a Black man's success. All we could do was promise that we wouldn't make the same mistakes he thought he had made. That was a long time ago.

Isaac looked at his gas meter again to see that the needle was now on empty. "I sure hope Dad left me some money, because I only have five dollars to my name, and I have to have some gas for this raggedy car!"

As Isaac pulled into the gas station, he began thinking about what it would be like to have a new car. If his father had left him enough money, he would buy a brand new car. If his father had not left him much, he would get a good used car. If there was not enough for a car, he would buy some new clothes, especially some suits since he would need interview suits upon graduation.

"But what if the preacher-man left here with nothing?" he thought. "That is out of the realm of possibilities, because Dad knew Mom doesn't make much money and hasn't worked full-time in nearly twenty years. He wouldn't leave Mom without any dough! That's right, and Mom would then give me and Ishmael some for school, and what's left over, we can use for whatever we want!"

Isaac began to savor the thought of having thousands of dollars of play money and how happy he would be to have that kind of financial freedom or license to not feel limited or constrained in any way. Isaac, excited about his father's estate, finished pumping the gas, and drove off toward home.

The Street Reports, November 7 – IS Financial Services recommended that investors buy ACBN at $24 per share and predicted it would increase in price to $30 within 6 to 12 months because ACB Holdings had chosen a market niche that should show above-average growth.

Positive or negative predictions of stock prices are reflections of market perception rather than of real financial facts. Changes in price i.e., price movement reflects ever-changing perceptions of value as evidenced in the current supply and demand.

The Discovery

It was early in November. Townley Street looked different today. The tree-lined street that usually had children running up and down it seemed eerily quiet. The clouds had lingered just a little too long to prevent the sun from casting its glow.

"Is this the street I used to rip up and down on?" Isaac wondered.

It seemed unwelcoming, and that was strange because coming home was always a small celebration. Reverend Jamison and Julene always prepared a dinner full of Isaac's favorites. "Straight-ahead" jazz would be wafting from upstairs, and Reverend Jamison would be ready to present his son with a self-recorded cassette tape of the newest in progressive jazz. Over dinner they discussed business classes at school, and then they would go out for dessert. His father would always say, "It's so good to have you home."

"It's good to be home," Isaac thought as he pulled into the driveway. Isaac was excited to see his mother and twin, but saddened that there would be no jazz, no tapes and no father greeting him at the door.

Ishmael met Isaac at the door. Whenever they were face to face, they were taken aback not so much by their identical features, but that they also looked so much like their father. Ishmael was glad to see his brother, and Isaac was relieved that Ishmael was able to be with their mother before he arrived.

"I have something for you," Ishmael said. He handed Isaac a tape titled *My Favorite Things*. "Dad made this for you before he died."

Isaac's eyes filled with tears. And naturally, whenever one of the twins cried, the other one would too.

"It's about time you got here. Ishmael and I were just about to eat your..." their mother paused for dramatic effect, "...macaroni and cheese!"

Isaac was relieved and appreciative, that they tried to welcome him home just as his father would have. "Thanks Mom, thanks Ishmael. I...I... "

"It's strange not having your father here, believe me, I know, but sometimes I feel as if he is here, do y'all know what I mean?" asked Julene.

Isaac and Ishmael looked at each other with skepticism but knew that they should encourage their mother to find comfort anyway she could. "Yes, Mom," they said in unison.

"Yes, well, I wish he were here right now to explain all this paperwork to us!"

From one side of the eight-person dining room table, she pushed a box full of paper toward her sons who always sat next to each other, across the table from their parents. "Why don't you two look this over while I pour you some drinks?" Julene pushed away from the table and walked over to the refrigerator. The twins began looking through the shoebox.

"Mom," Ishmael said teasingly, "Isaac can figure this out; he's a business major!" Isaac shot him a look that could kill. "Man, I don't understand this stuff!"

"There's not much here to understand," Ishmael offered. "Let me see." He pulled out a piece of paper that read:

CONFIRMATION

Thomas Securities
B.B. Freeman, Broker
1423 Appian Street
Houston, TX 45679
713-444-9874
October 22, 1991

Acct: #5678-23-9665
Marcus Jamison
6768 Townley Street
Houston, TX 45678
SS# 333-33-3000

Position	Shares	Company	Purchase Price	Balance
Long	4,200	ACBN	23.50	$98,700

Julene returned to the table with drinks and chips on a serving tray. "So what do you think all this means?"

"I really don't know what this is Mom," replied Ishmael, "but it looks like Dad invested about $100,000, apparently just before he died. I wonder if..."

Isaac, furious with what he saw, yelled, "I know exactly what this is about! It's about Dad being full of crap!"

Ishmael and Julene were shocked, for they had never seen Isaac throw a temper tantrum, let alone ever say anything negative about his father.

"Fool, I'll slap the..." Julene threatened, fearful that she might actually hit Isaac. Ishmael rushed to stand between them for fear that his mother might deepen wounds that he knew existed as a result of Isaac's relationship with their dad.

"Mom, please sit down now. And Isaac, man, shut up!"

"Man, you know Dad was full of it, and now there's proof!"

Isaac mumbled under his breath, "Cheap and poor!"

Julene rose from her chair again, but this time with a calm and steely demeanor. Her sons were now embroiled in a heated argument about whether their dad was a good man, a good husband, a good father, or neither - as if being there for them everyday for twenty years was worth less than the ninety-eight thousand dollars he left upon his death. As she approached them, she saw now what they saw in themselves: the two Marcuses she knew. One was spiritual and self-righteous; the other enjoyed business success and money. For twenty-two years, she had lived with and counseled the man torn between the two lives. Now, she had to deal with identical twin sons, different in opinion and both like their father.

Trusting that they would never physically cause real harm to each other, she watched them as they pushed each other with each retort. It was as if one young Marcus had returned to resolve old conflicts between his religious and secular selves. Lord knows he left not having resolved the two, Julene thought.

"Dad was here, he provided for us, and he was good to others. What more would you want in a man?" Ishmael argued as he pushed Isaac.

"Man, if Dad had been all that great of a man, he would have left a whole lot more for his wife and children." There was silence. "You know I'm right! He spent so much time preaching about the evils of money that he nearly convinced himself that he didn't need it, oh, with the exception of his salary, which came before church improvements. Yeah, he didn't need money for his family, but he needed a nice house to entertain his flock, and his flock wanted him to have nice things, but no one helped him set up a pension plan. So, you know what I say? I say, forget the church! Where's the survivor's annuity for Mom? Huh? Where is that?!" There was more silence.

Ishmael stopped pushing his twin. He stood there confused, because he did not understand why $98,000 was not enough (it was certainly more than he was expecting). Julene began to cry. Isaac knew he had said the wrong thing. He turned to his mother to apologize, but she was already leaving the dining room.

"Mom!" Isaac cried, "I'm sorry," and he ran after her.

Ishmael, with his arms crossed, walked over to the stove where the teapot had been whistling during their argument. As Ishmael made a cup of tea for his mother, he began to wonder whether Isaac might have been right. Would his mother be well off? His father might not have left enough money for his mother, or maybe he did not know enough about his father to make that kind of judgment. Reaching for the statement that started the argument in the first place, Ishmael decided that the best thing he could do was to call the stranger whose name appeared on the statement: B.B. Freeman.

First Visit With B.B.

There was just enough room for seven people in the dimly lit, old-fashioned elevator. As they went up, the cranking of the pulley left Julene, Ishmael and Isaac feeling a little unsure about whether they were in the right building.

"I thought those financial types worked in really nice places," Julene whispered to Isaac.

"Me too, Mom," Isaac replied, embarrassed that, with all his fancy business education, he had never seen a financial advisor or visited a brokerage office.

"Achoo!" Someone sneezed so hard that the elevator shook.

"We're almost there," Ishmael assured his family, though he was not sure he really wanted to meet this mysterious B.B. Freeman, except to take the money and deposit it in a more reputable looking office.

As the elevator approached the seventh floor, the Jamisons' nervousness increased. They were apprehensive about meeting someone who had more power over their family's money than they did. How did they know B.B. Freeman could be trusted? What if B.B. Freeman were some guy who talked a lot of financial gobbledygook just to confuse them, rendering them powerless and him (it was probably a man, most of those financial types were) more powerful? They were all feeling skeptical, as they stared silently at a wall plaque next to a frosted glass door:

B.B. Freeman, Stockbroker
Thomas Securities

The Jamisons looked at each other with relief and some doubt.

"Is B.B. Freeman a security guard too?" Ishmael asked. Isaac looked at his twin in amazement that in some ways they could be so vastly different.

"Security guard?! Man, securities are investments: stocks and bonds and stuff." Confident that Ishmael could not lead the discussion and that his mother would defer to any man who possessed the ability to talk financial jargon, Isaac continued, "Mom, just let me handle this. I'm a business major."

Ishmael stood still in his own ignorance that he had mistaken Thomas Securities for a security guard office. One point for Isaac, he thought.

Isaac opened the door to find a cramped, one-room office with two desks, papers strewn across a table, one computer and one typewriter, a wall of file cabinets, dingy yellowish-brown wallpaper and two people.

The woman said, "Yes, can we help you?"

"I'm Isaac Jamison, Pastor Marcus Jamison's son. This is my mother Julene Jamison and my brother Ishmael who called you to set up an appointment with B.B. Freeman." Ishmael and his mother were surprised to see Isaac act so business-like, as he more often than not, acted like a fool around them.

The woman replied, "Why don't y'all have a seat and Mr. Freeman will be with you in a moment."

While searching for a third chair that was not too dusty, they began to wonder whether they had just entered the twilight zone. An old man in white shirt sleeves with a wrinkled collar, presumably Mr. Freeman, sat a mere four feet from the woman, yet was working with his back to her as if he were in a different room.

"Mr. Freeman, The Jamisons, your 3:00 is here."

He looked at his watch, turned around to thank her, and then turned around to face the Jamisons, "So, you must be Pastor Marcus Jamison's family. Is that right?"

No one wanted to admit that they were who they actually were because upon examining Mr. Freeman and his surroundings, they could not see how someone of his appearance could be one of those "financial types."

Freeman stood up, stretched out his hand to Isaac and said, "Ishmael, I'm so glad you called."

"Thank you, Mr. Freeman, but I'm Isaac," responded Isaac. "We're identical twins, as you can see." The problem was that Mr. Freeman could not see very well through his rather thick lenses.

"I see," Mr. Freeman said as he peered over his glasses at Isaac, then at Ishmael, then back at Isaac, then back at Ishmael. Meanwhile Julene prayed that this man was legitimate. Freeman gestured for them to have a seat.

A cheap stockbroker, thought Isaac. He was convinced that this old man in his cheap, ugly digs, half-blind and modestly dressed, could not know much about investing in the White domain of high finance. If he was all that successful his office would have been downtown, nicely decorated, and they would not be scrounging for chairs.

"Mr. Freeman," Isaac said, "thank you for agreeing to meet with us on such short notice. I don't know if you were aware that my father died and left in his safe deposit box this statement that has your name on it."

"I was saddened to hear about Marcus's death. He was a good man…" Freeman's voice trailed off.

"We don't know what to make of it, at least not fully, but I, we, thought to give you a call to discuss it with you." Ishmael handed the statement to Freeman. Isaac continued, "Sir, we have reason to believe our father left us more than that and wanted to know where the rest is?" Julene wondered where that comment came from, but would never dream of asking Isaac to hold his

A corporation raises capital (i.e., money) through the sale of shares of stock. Each share represents an ownership in the corporation and is a claim on the corporation's earnings and assets. It usually entitles the shareholder to vote in the election of directors and on other matters taken up at shareholder meetings. **Common stock** allows the shareholder certain rights, but **preferred stock** gets paid dividends before the common. **Dividends** are a distribution of earnings (or profits) to the shareholders.

tongue. She silently hoped there was more money.

"Really?" Freeman asked curiously.

"We don't know what we have. That's why we're here," Julene added, and Ishmael nodded in agreement. "Mr. Freeman," Julene continued, "what does this statement mean?"

Freeman looked at the statement very intensely, as if he had to figure it out himself. He turned it around then pulled out his magnifying glass. "It looks like you might have everything you need…" his voice trailed off.

"Excuse me, but how can $98,000 be all that we need?! You can't even live on that much in a year!" said Isaac.

"Who said anything about $98,000?" asked Freeman. "What you have are 4,200 shares of ACBN." Freeman turned to his computer, punched a few keys, and then turned the computer screen their way. "Currently, at $16.00 a share, your account is valued at $67, 200. But don't worry."

The Jamisons were shocked. Isaac jumped from his chair and angrily demanded an explanation from Freeman.

B.B rose from his chair, "I want to thank you all for coming in today. Please call again when you want to know more."

"But Mr. Freeman," cried Julene, "what are we supposed to do with this? We don't know what it is."

"It's a stock investment in Ashanti Cable Broadcasting Network. Do nothing until I give you the signal. Right now, you have everything you need. Now if you'll excuse me?"

The Jamison family rose to their feet and left the office. As they waited for the elevator, Ishmael asked Isaac, "Was that your idea of being in charge, my brother?"

Less Than Favorable Rating

The cranking noise seemed unbearable now. "Can you imagine Dad investing his money with B.B. Freeman? What did he see in that old, no-seeing, no-hearing, weird-talking-supposed-to-be stock broker?" Isaac demanded of the ceiling.

"I'm not sure," muttered Ishmael, "but I'm going back there alone the next time."

"Why, brother?"

"Because twin, you offended the man and then all of a sudden he didn't have time for us. I had asked him for two hours of his time because I thought we could benefit from a little lesson in investments. Instead all we got was a 'you have everything you need, and do nothing until I tell you to.' What did you learn from *that*?"

"I learned that I'm taking my share of the money elsewhere and would suggest you and Mom do the same."

Julene was angry. "What if I don't give you one cent!? What will you do then? What if I keep it all to myself for back wages for taking care of you two for 21 years?"

"But Mom, why would you, knowing that Dad would have wanted his sons to have some?"

"Did your Dad leave a will? No! Therefore, you really don't know what he wanted, do you? No! No! No! So don't even try that 'Dad would have wanted stuff' with me, because if you were that concerned about what Dad would have wanted, you'd be spending more time in church!" Julene did not want to pull rank, but knew that if she did not Isaac would sweet-talk her into changing her mind.

The rickety elevator finally reached the lobby. "Isaac, I don't want to hear another word from you about this money until I bring it up. In the meantime, I suggest you call the financial aid office to find out what you need to do to pay for school."

Isaac was shocked. What he thought was his obviously was not guaranteed. Not being stupid, he knew that if he were to get anything, he would have to obey his mother's wishes. Ishmael watched as his twin struggled to fake a smile. "Okay, Mom. I'll wait until you bring it up again."

Julene smiled, not because she intended to keep the money for herself, but because she wanted to convey a message – begging, whining and grubbing would not work. She did not mind playing on Isaac's fears, but she had a dilemma. On the one hand, if she gave Ishmael (the less materialistic son) any money, she would have to give Isaac an equal amount. On the other hand, she wanted to make sure that Isaac understood that money does not make the man. Ultimately, learning about money could be one last rite of passage for her sons before they began earning their own money. Julene, now a widow, faced the inevitable, that her sons would soon need her less. To her surprise, she began to feel relief.

Julene Breaks Down

"The Retreat" is what Marcus and Julene called their bedroom. It was the one place that was off limits to everyone they knew, even their sons. There was no phone, no photographs of other people, no objects that formerly belonged to other people. They did not even open the blinds. The only decorations were a few souvenirs from places they had traveled together and a large portrait taken on their wedding day.

When they bought the house fifteen years ago, it did not look the way it did now. Julene remembered telling Marcus that if they purchased the home, it would have to be redecorated immediately. Marcus did not argue; he just asked her how much money she would need and gave it to her.

First, the layers of wallpaper were removed, and the walls were painted off-white. Then, the bare hardwood floors were carpeted with a deep blue lushness that brought a regal air to the room. Julene had wanted new bedroom furniture for some time, but had not wanted to furnish their old apartment with nice furniture. "It would look out of place!" she would often say. But with their own house, she was in the right place for the right kind of furniture. While Marcus was away on a business trip, she purchased an entire bedroom suite consisting of a walnut, king-sized bed, matching nightstands, dresser with mirror, and a bureau.

When Marcus returned, he was pleasantly surprised and grateful that his wife of five years knew his taste and decorated "The Retreat" accordingly. That evening, under the quilts made by Julene's grandmother, they expressed their love, passion, and commitment to stay together, in love, forever and ever.

Weary from the weight of daydreams of Marcus, Julene asked herself "Why didn't anyone tell me that forever only lasted twenty-five years?" She rose from the bed three hours past her normal work-out-clean-up-and-visit-with-friends routine. Three hours was precious time that she could not afford to spend with others.

Julene had had enough of friends, family, co-workers, and people in general. During the first few weeks after Marcus' death, it was as if she could not get away from people, especially church members. They came by practically hourly to pray with her, for her, about her and with their hands on her.

"Dear Lord, we ask thee for thy blessings on Mrs. Jamison and her sons, Isaac and Ishmael."

"Yes, Lord," someone else would shout.

"Lord, we thank you for Reverend Jamison and the legacy he left on his flock and family."

"Yes, Lord." It would go on and on like that for an hour in the morning, afternoon, and early evening. After three weeks of prayers, Julene began to ask Jesus if she could just have a moment's silence to grieve properly.

Today, Jesus must have answered her prayers, for shortly after she finished her workout, she began crying. If only Isaac could see me now, she thought. Fearing her neighbors would hear her, she closed the windows and wailed into the pillow where her beloved had once laid his head. She cried louder and louder the more she thought about the twenty-some years they had slept together, cuddled closely together during the cold nights, and even closer together during the warm nights. The more she cried, the more she remembered her fears of losing his love. Now, she feared, she had not loved him enough.

As she sobbed, her tears and thoughts seemed uncontrollable. She heard laughter, deep laughter, sweet whispers, God-inspired shouting, babies crying, gospel music, all the moments that their lives revolved around, until she heard, "Dad should have done more for you, Mom." Like others who have lost their loved ones prematurely, Julene was certainly angry with Marcus for leaving her suddenly. She blamed God on occasion, asking, "Why does it seem as if You always take the good ones?" So, she was surprised that she felt justified in entertaining Isaac's suggestion that *the* Reverend Marcus Jamison was not all that great of a man because he only left $98,000 to his family.

Julene had always had a special way of seeing both sides of an issue, especially when it came to seeing herself. She reckoned that it was normal to be angry at her beloved for dying unexpectedly, but not to be angry for leaving her just $98,000. Why? They had never discussed money before, not in a real way in which they decided how much they would leave each other and the kids should something happen to one of them. Death had not been part of the plan.

"I wonder why he didn't tell me he had $98,000 all those times I said we needed to do this or that, or go here or there, or buy this or that. All he would say is, 'we have everything we need, when you think about it. Hasn't God provided everything anyone could possibly need?' Sometimes she resented Marcus' bringing God into the buying decision, for who could say "no" to God? Julene could not argue with Marcus. For all she knew, if she had food, clothing, shelter, his love and the love of her sons, she really did not need anything else, whether God provided it or not.

Because she thought less about money than her husband had, she realized that she was grateful for what he had left. Yes, he was a good man. Yes, she had loved him as much as her heart would let her. Nothing scared her more than the fear of never loving him again. With that, she began sobbing again, without concern for who might hear her. She cried with the hope that someone might actually hear her, and rescue her from the pain – not with prayers this time, but with assurances that a forty-five year-old widow without a career could make it on her own.

As the day passed, no one heard her, and no one came. Then the phone rang. She looked at the clock and picked up the phone. It was Ishmael, always attentive, calling to reassure her that everything would be fine. With that consolation, she stopped crying, said goodnight to her more sensitive son, and fell asleep.

Twins Get Their Own

For the first time in weeks, there was a little excitement in the air. The twins were happy to be home for the weekend, relaxing with their mother who had called them home so that she could make an important announcement. Julene had made a decision about the stocks.

"Sons, listen to me very carefully. I've decided what I want to do with the money your father left." She paused. "I've given it a lot of thought, and I'm firm in my decision. If either of you argues with me, I will take the stock back from you and keep it for myself. Do you understand?"

"What's not to understand?" Isaac asked, "Just give me my money – please."

"Now hold your horses. Before I announce what I'm doing, I want to explain my rationale. You're both almost twenty-one, adults. Soon, you'll be college graduates and pursuing your careers. Your dad did a terrific job helping you understand what it means to be men, and I think I did a great job of nurturing you along the way. You're both good at what you do, your grades are good, and you're good problem solvers. As much as I loved your father, I think he confused you both in that he was part angel and part shrewd entrepreneur. He didn't do a good job of reconciling his two sides, so he taught you Isaac, one side, and taught you Ishmael, the other. As a consequence, my genetically identical twins are fraternal twins philosophically. You can both learn a lot from each other.

"So, here it is. I had thought about splitting it evenly since there are three of us, and that would have made it simple. Then, I thought about giving you both a lot, and keeping a little bit for myself, because you're so young, and the more you have, the better start in the real world you would have. Then, I thought about keeping most of it for myself, but then I thought no, that would be greedy."

"That's right, Mom!" Isaac said.

"But, then I thought, it's not about who gets how much, it's about the lesson that giving and getting stock comes with. So here it is."

"What?" Ishmael and Isaac said impatiently, for once in total agreement.

"Your Dad and I have paid, to date, $90,000 for your college education. You've each paid nothing up till now. You both need only about $15,000 each to pay all your expenses senior year. With your father's death, we've just lost about 85% of our family income. So, I think it's time you both began financially supporting your own needs and wants. I'm giving you both $5,000 in stock, not because I think it will help you with school expenses all that much, but because I want you to have just enough stock to learn how to invest – to test whether you can learn to make the most of your money – and stop spending mine. The day after you graduate, let's compare our accounts to see who's learned the most about investing. At that time, I may give you more money, based on what you've done in your accounts". Julene looked into her sons' faces to read their true reactions. For a moment, she only saw Marcus. "So what do you two think?" Julene asked, proud of herself for sharing and doubly proud of her husband for providing, even after his death.

Ishmael and Isaac were visibly shocked.

"So?" she insisted.

Isaac looked at Ishmael who looked back. For a moment, they were locked in a stare.

Ishmael rose to his feet and hugged his mother, then said, "Mom, I want you to have it. If Dad had wanted us, I mean, me to have it, then he would have opened an account in my name. You keep it."

"No, your father left it to me to decide what to do, and I'm going to share it with you two. You're old enough to decide what to do with it after that."

"Mother," said Isaac, "that's a sound decision you made, encouraging us to learn how to invest our own money, but I have one question. In school we learned that real investment success is made on larger sums of money. I'm afraid you won't be able to determine whether we are good investors with only $5,000 in stock to reinvest. Consider this example. I invest $5,000 and at the end of the year, if I do well by earning about ten percent, I will have made $500. If I had $15,000, and invested it the same way, I will have made $1,500. Wouldn't you rather choose that option?"

Julene was reminded of Marcus, the businessman. She could always count on Isaac to present his most desired option in that business tone that no one could refute. Cognizant that Isaac was terribly serious about his business presentation, she slowly lifted her hand to her mouth to hide the smile erupting from her face, but she could only contain her laughter for so long.

"Isaac," she said in a curious tone, "if I invest the same amount of money you invest in the same way, would you come out better just because the money is in your account?"

"Of course not!" Isaac said, feeling set-up.

"Well, then, if you're such a good investor, I'll give you a year to prove it before I give you more. I've arranged another meeting with B.B. Freeman for next Saturday. He knows you're both in school and can't meet during the week. Can y'all come back for that?"

"Have him send me my paperwork. I don't want to go up in that old man Freeman's office again; he's weird. Whatever this 'B.B.' knows," Isaac said with a sneer, "I can learn it myself, and then some. Ishmael, man, you're not going to use that brother are you? He's…"

"I know, strange, but don't you want to give the brother a chance?" replied Ishmael. "I mean, you're judging him on appearances alone. Think about it. Who's the toughest business-man you know? Dad. And if Dad used him, why shouldn't we?"

An Old Story

B.B. Freeman had not built a business on arrogance and gloating, but today, he was savoring the Jamison family meeting.

"Welcome back, Julene. It's so good to see you and your wonderful sons again." B.B. rushed to start, "I understand that we have about two hours together for me to explain how the stock market works and advise you as to whether you should keep ACBN or invest in something else. It took three years before Reverend Jamison took my advice to invest, so I don't expect his sons will come to take my advice in two hours. Nevertheless, I want to make sure you, Julene, understand how to work your money and not let your money work you."

Turning to Ishmael and Isaac, B.B. continued, "Boys, I know I don't look like the guys you see on t.v., but I used to – when impressing others was important to me." He paused to see if the twins caught his inference. "You see, there is a reason why we Black folks don't know as much as we should about investing – it's because we refuse to listen. If you don't want to listen, then please leave now."

"Mr. Freeman, I want to hear what you have to say, but I'm going to invest my own way," Isaac informed him.

"Fair enough. Now, call me B.B." And B.B. proceeded to educate.

"My great, great, grandfather, Tobi Johnston, one of the many slaves of Franklin Johnston, III, used to gather his children around the fire to tell them stories about how to prosper in America, should they ever escape slavery or be freed. He would take a stick or a knife or use his finger, and draw this." With hands shaking as if he had drunk a gallon of coffee, B.B. swiftly drew something, turned the paper around, and motioned for the Jamisons to move toward his desk.

"What is this?" Ishmael asked.

"What does it look like to you?" B.B. replied.

"Had you asked me, I would have said it looks like a picture of that foil Christmas tree Mom and Dad had at the apartment!" Isaac said, laughing.

"Why are you wasting away in business school with comedic talent like that?" B.B. was tiring already. "I'm no artist for sure…"

Isaac wondered whether B.B. was actually a stockbroker.

"But if you look carefully, this is a plant. There are the leaves, stems, branches, of course, the pods, the bolls, roots and over here, floating in the air, are the seeds."

"Cotton?" Julene asked in surprise.

"Mr. Freeman, I mean, B.B.," Ishmael began, "I don't mean any disrespect, but why are you drawing us a picture of a cotton plant, when we are here to talk about my mother's account?"

"Now that's a good question. I thought you wanted to know how to make the most of your money." The surviving Jamison family all looked at each other. B.B. watched them and anticipated that in their silence, they would gang up on him as so many other Black families had done in the past. He sat there wondering whether they had the ability to just listen for once, rather than telling him how to do his job.

"B.B.," Isaac announced in his very businesslike tone, "I see that once again, I'm going to have to take the lead here. We're not here for stories, and we're really not here for advice. We're not asking you to tell us whether Mom should keep the money. She has already decided what she will do. All we need right now is for you to show *me* how to transfer *my* money to another account. Do you understand?"

"Perfectly," B.B. responded, happy professionally, but hurt personally. "Your new broker will help you transfer your money over. Thank you for the opportunity to serve your investment needs. You may leave now."

Julene and Ishmael were stunned by Isaac's assertiveness and equally stunned that B.B. did not seem desperate for their business, especially given that he did not appear to make much money.

Isaac got up from his chair and left the office. "I'll be waiting in the car."

"As I was saying," B.B. continued as if Isaac's rude outburst

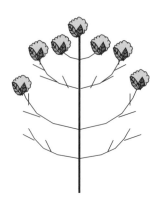 never happened, "there is the plant, the leaves, stems, the flower, branches, pods, seeds, roots, bolls and, of course, the lint. If you look at the branches, you will notice that each branch goes upward. This is a good plant. But many cotton plants looked like this –"

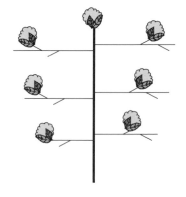

"Most of the folks picking cotton would pick from these branches because they were easier to find than the others. That's human nature. The problem was, the cotton on these plants was of a lesser quality. Folk would even pick cotton from the branches that nearly went sideways, like these –"

"The branches didn't go up, they just kind of laid there, struggling to grow upward.

"Now, Tobi really didn't want to know how to pick the best cotton, but he knew that when faced with the option of picking

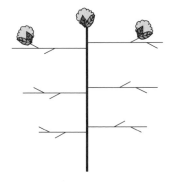

cotton or starving, he should pick from the best plants. Thereby earning the most money for the quality of his harvest. Tobi learned early on that steady growth, represented by straight branches pointing upwards, meant more money, faster. Let me repeat that, slowly. Steady growth, represented by straight branches pointing upwards, meant more money, faster. There was never any question that Tobi knew what to pick.

"He often dreamed of poisoning cotton, but knew it would be like killing himself – not an option with a family to care for. Yes, Tobi would dream of drought, for without the rain, the cotton couldn't grow. If his prayers were answered, not only would the cotton die, but so would he. He dreamed of pestilence, but again, that meant certain death for those who depended on 'King Cotton.'

"Tobi would constantly tell other slaves how to pick cotton. They would argue that he was doing the slave owner's work by teaching them something they had absolutely no interest in. He would argue that it is better to learn the fundamentals of what's valuable, so that they could survive *after* slavery. Now let me repeat that slowly. It's better to learn the fundamentals of what's valuable so you can survive after dependency on your employer."

B.B. paused and looked intently at Julene and Ishmael. "Nothing grows without rain, without nourishment, and when I say nothing, I mean your money, too. Even money needs rain…more money…to grow. Are you following me?" They shook their heads affirmatively.

B.B. continued, "Tobi dreamed of drought, pestilence and armed rebellion. The conditions were such that you had to fight silently in your head. Or die. The way the slaves fought back was to decide on the cruelest land owners, pretend that they were planting cottonseeds on a timely basis, but actually plant them later to reduce the size of the crop. If the plants bloomed in the early spring, the soil would have been too cold for the roots to function, damaging the stem."

"Can you imagine what it was like to be a Negro slave in the South back then?" With a faraway look in his eyes, B.B. continued the story.

One of Tobi's sons, Thomas Johnston, was obedient to his father. If his father said anything that Thomas disagreed with, Thomas would obey anyway because he believed that Tobi knew more about life because he had lived longer and that God bestowed wisdom on fathers. He remembered Tobi telling him that one day there would be no more slavery and that he was preparing the men for the day when they would have to work for themselves, not anyone else.

Tobi often said, "Do you think there will be cotton after slavery?" Most would agree that there was the possibility. "Then you best get to learning how to pick the best 'cause the best cotton pickers are going to be the best prepared to care for themselves after we escape or are freed."

Because Tobi taught Thomas the secret of the cotton plant branches, there was never any question that he knew what to pick. "Look for the ripest of bolls. When you find

*them, you'll see nothing but flowering branches on the main
stem. If you see that, then you know that those branches can
feed all the flowers. Now that's the best kind of plant there
is."*

Times changed and slavery, the cruel institution, came
to an end and left many slaves to wonder what next? Thomas, schooled and skilled in cotton picking, knew that there
was more than one cotton farmer he could offer his services
to. For obvious reasons he did not like Master Johnston;
therefore he offered his services to another farmer, DeVrees.
DeVrees was new to the South, having come from the North
to get rich off the backs of cheap sharecropper labor.

Thomas also preferred working for DeVrees because he
represented the group of White people that had freed the Negroes. DeVrees had a soft manner and lots of fancy ways. He
looked like he was able to pay on time, too. Still, Thomas
was skeptical. He knew not to agree to any contract DeVrees
might offer, because it meant sure slavery in the end. No
matter how fair of a man DeVrees was if you worked the land
under contract, you belonged to the land. If the land was
sold, you were obligated to work the land, no matter who
owned it.

Thomas dreamt about having his own land and the privileges ownership bestowed. If he had his own land, it would
come with a lot of privileges. He had these thoughts often
but rarely shared them with anyone. One time he mentioned
to his friends his dreams of owning land, and they laughed at
him. He could not understand the laughter, until he realized
they laughed because they thought he wanted to be some-

thing he could not be: White.

"Just because you aren't a slave doesn't mean you can own land!" they said. "How many freedmen do you know owning land? How much do you think land costs?"

Thomas would sit in bewilderment that they had no ability to see things changing, at least not in their lifetimes. Then he remembered that his father had prepared him for the day he would not be a slave, even during slavery. Thomas said once, and only once, "DeVrees told me that if I was to ever do better than I can do right now, then I best get me some land."

His friends fell silent, and then one said, "So you want land because the White man told you you should have it?"

But Thomas was not discouraged because he knew that it would take a while before the others could see past slavery. Their problem was that even if the 'White Man' made sense, they would do just the opposite, for the White Man had become the embodiment of all nonsense, at best, and evil, at worst. Thomas understood the sentiment. After all, how could he say anything good about a people who would en-slave others for hundreds of years?

"Thomas!" his friend Maxi shouted while trying to hold back his laughter, "Now, what if you were to go about get-ting you some land. When would you get it, from where, for how much, and what would you do with it?"

Thomas could not tell if Maxi were making a serious in-quiry or just testing him. "I'm not quite sure!"

His friends laughed, and Maxi said, "In these times, you want to be sure of what you're doing, and you have to know how to do it. You don't get no second chances, and you don't have no slavery to fall back on, so the best thing you can do is the surest thing, and that is work somebody else's land, and get paid, and go on about your life. Just think, if you had your own land, who would pay you to work it? Nobody! So, you best just work somebody else's land."

For the first time Thomas was challenged to consider whether his objective was merely a wild fantasy. It was true that if he owned the land himself, no one would pay him any-thing—not money, not even plantation store vouchers.

"Thomas, how do you think we doubled our pay in one year? As long as we aren't the landowners, we got to de-mand more pay. We have worked all of our lives without money, and every chance we get, we gonna ask for more, and more and more and more."

Thomas nodded in agreement, although he knew they would never have their own land because they did not see the value in ownership. He could not argue with the fact that they should be paid more because he felt he should be paid more too – hence, DeVrees.

Being the odd man out, Thomas responded, "Maxi, have you ever asked ole man Johnston if he'd let you buy a plot?"

Maxi turned to their friends and they all laughed, harder than before. In all their laughter, they had failed to ask Thomas if he would ever ask DeVrees for the opportunity to buy some property.

"B.B., where are you going with all this?" Julene asked impatiently.

"Remember your promise," B.B. chided. "All you have to do is sit and listen. When the meeting is done, you decide whether you want to work with me or not." B.B. returned to his story.

"Johan DeVrees!" DeVrees said as he answered the knock on his door.

"It's Thomas Johnston, sir."

DeVrees opened the door and invited Thomas in with a motion. It was a familiar gesture that said, take two steps in, but stop there. Thomas entered just past the door and stood there in deference to DeVrees's landowner privilege.

"Mr. DeVrees, our relationship has been very good," Thomas began, "I've picked the best cotton first and the worst, last. You have paid me well, and I have been satisfied. I've noticed lately though, that you have a plot of land with more bad cotton plants than good."

"Oh, really?" DeVrees, in his ignorance, said.

"Yes, sir. I couldn't really figure out why you come so far to buy land with a mostly bad crop. If you don't mind my asking, who in the world sold you that land?"

"Johnston," DeVrees confessed.

"Mr. Johnston! You know, my family was once belonging to Mr. Johnston. Why do you think I work for you and not him? Because he hardly has any good cotton to pick and if you can't pick no good cotton, and you're a sharecropper, you'd best find something else to do."

Thomas told him story after story of how the cottonseed was planted too late, how it was not irrigated properly. He also threw in a few tales of how the slaves would dance around the fire yelling and screaming to their many African gods to bring on a drought and kill the cotton – and it worked.

After Thomas finished storytelling, he stated, "Now, Mr. DeVrees. I can fix your land. I've been fixing bad crops all my life, from sun up to sun down, every day of the week. If you want me to try to fix your land, I'm going to have to charge you more because there is nothing good for me to pick."

DeVrees asked, "How do I know that if I pay you more that you can actually fix it?"

"You know, I've worked most of my life as a slave. I don't have any money but the money I make from you. I cannot guarantee you that your crop can be repaired. It might be damaged too much. I will try my hardest, but it won't be fixed soon. I'm going to need time, about a year."

"But you can leave whenever you want. If you want more money, you're going to have to sign a contract that you will work this land for a year. Would you be willing to do that?" DeVrees asked.

Thomas stood quiet for a moment, then said, "Mr. DeVrees. I don't know if I want to make the same mistake you made by tying myself to land that might not be very useful. I think you got taken 'cause you're from the North with fancy ways. I'm guessing that you don't know much about how cotton grows. Now you have a lot of land that you paid good money for, and you may not be able to make much from it. Let me try this. You pay me $200 for getting your land in shape, and I'll sign a one-year contract because I know that the land will be in better shape after I'm done. If I don't *repair the land as best as it can be repaired, I will take on that ole nasty plot myself, and pay you back $200."*

DeVrees began to pace back and forth, then he circled Thomas. Thomas began to sweat a little. Then he began to cry.

"Why are you crying?!" DeVrees shouted.

"I'm crying because I feel guilty. You're a good man, Mr. DeVrees, a fair man who got some bad land because we tried to get back at Mr. Johnston. We ruined his land. If I have to be burdened with that land for the rest of my life, then so be it!"

DeVrees, convinced, and now angry that he got a bad deal, looked at Thomas and said, "Thomas, you're right. I am a fair man. You should not have set out to destroy anyone's property, no matter how you were treated. If I weren't so mad at Johnston, I'd turn you in to the authorities, but since I am fair, you should be burdened yourself with the land that you and those criminal slaves destroyed. I will pay you $150."
He paused. "I'm not sure if I can trust you on this Thomas. I know the land is bad, so let me ask you this: Would you buy that land if you had enough money?"

Thomas, wiping his tears with his sleeve, bugged his eyes at DeVrees and said, "Now sir, you know I can't own no land! Even if I could, I wouldn't buy bad land."

"Thomas, that little plot you're so worried about would probably go for about $1,000 in the condition it's in. I don't think anyone down here is going to buy it, so I'll tell you what I'm going to do. I'm not giving you $200 to the fix the land. I'm giving you $150 to fix the land in one year. You'd better

do whatever you can to fix it. If you don't fix it, you will have to buy that land from me for $1,000. Is that understood?" DeVrees asked as if it was all his idea.

Noticing how DeVrees had taken ownership of Thomas' idea, Thomas answered, "Mr. DeVrees, I like the way you think."

"Thomas, for the first time in his life, felt like a free man, and consequently changed the family name from Johnston to Freeman." B.B. felt accomplished. It had been a long time since he told that story. Every other client had cut him off before he could finish it. Now, he felt as if he had made a significant impact on the way Julene and Ishmael would understand investing in the stock market.

"So, do you get it now?" he asked.

Julene and Ishmael looked at each other, and Ishmael said, "Mr. Freeman, thank you for that. We really appreciate your time and effort. Speaking for myself, I think we should end our meeting now, think about what you said, and get back with you about what we want to do."

B.B. was surprised, though he should not have been. Every other time he tried to tell the story, he promised himself that it would be the last time. He hated failure, but more than that, he hated to see Black folks disinterested in the success stories of other Black folks, especially his family.

"I understand," B.B. said. "Julene, what would you like to do with your stock?"

Julene was taken aback by B.B.'s direct approach. To her, it seemed as if he had lost his patience, but what she did not know is that he was worried about whether she could make good investment decisions without Reverend Jamison.

Julene, still stunned by the question, closed her eyes as if she were in prayer. When she opened them, she looked straight at B.B. and asked, "Would you please advise me? I'm not really sure what stock is or how it works."

B.B. smiled in victory, but what he did not see at the time was that Julene was nervous. After all, Julene believed he was strange. He did not appear to be all that financially successful himself. He never gave a straight answer, and he liked to talk about off-the-subject topics like cotton plants. She wondered just then whether she had gotten herself into deep trouble by asking him to advise her.

B.B. asked Ishmael to step outside while he talked to Julene. Julene motioned to Ishmael that it was all right, "I'll be down in a minute. Why don't you keep Isaac company?"

Ishmael dutifully left, and B.B. proceeded to outline his terms for working with his clients. B.B. agreed to schedule time with her as long as her twin sons did not accompany her. He asked that Julene do what he advised her to do unless she had hard evidence or proof that his advice was not sound. She agreed, and they made an appointment to meet again.

B.B. walked from behind his desk, took Julene's hands in his and assured her that she would be fine. He thought that what she needed right now was assurance that she would not have to explore the world of finance alone. Julene's face did not convey complete trust and security, but he understood that she was going through a lot right now. In time, she would feel differently. After all, he had seen it happen to many women over the years.

As Julene left his office, B.B. returned to his desk. He turned off the computer, and pushed Reverend Jamison's file to the corner of his desk. He shook his head in wonderment about how Reverend Jamison could have invested all his money in stock without telling his family he was going to do it. Then, having died shortly after making the investment, he obviously had not had time to tell them what he had done. That was a strange thing that happened, B.B. thought.

In B.B.'s wonderment he found the answer to his question as to why the cotton plant story was so important. No one had ever really listened to his great, great, great grandfather, yet he turned out to be the wealthiest Black landowner in his county. B.B. thought it strange that no one had ever asked him, "Well, whatever happened to Thomas? Did he fix the land? Did he have to buy it from DeVrees? What did he do with the land?" No questions, no solutions, only literal interpretations on a simple slave story. B.B. promised himself one last time, "I'm never going to tell that story again."

ACB Events

The Street Reports, December 19 – Ashanti Broadcasting (ACBN) asked the New York Stock Exchange on December 18th to halt trading in its shares which dropped in share price by about 50% because nervous investors expressed concern about possible discrepancies in revenue and subscriber levels. ACB reported that their first quarter earnings were not up to analysts' expectations, but that earnings were up nonetheless. According to CEO Donald Jackson, investors and analysts "misunderstood" the difference between audience-level numbers compiled by Barnaby Viewcast Co. and its own subscriber figures. In Jackson's view, investors were confusing the Barnaby audience numbers with number of subscribers.

Tip: If a well-respected analyst estimates that a company's earnings should meet a particular estimate and it does not, it is possible that the stock price will drop until the issue is resolved. The stock price can also be negatively affected in the short run if an insider states that the stock price is overpriced, or a well-respected and credible outsider says something negative about a company.

Year 1

An uninformed decision begets unintended consequences.

Everyone Has An Opinion

"Hold on Mom while I conference you in," Isaac said as he punched a few buttons on his phone. "Twin, is that you?" Ishmael was glad to hear Isaac's voice.

"I have Mom on the phone. You know this is long distance, so let's try to keep it short. I'll start. I transferred my stock to Harry Smith Discount Brokers, then I sold it all immediately because it just kept going down and I don't think a Black-owned company catering only to Black folks who don't invest in stocks anyway is going to go up unless Black folks start investing in stocks *and* investing in ACBN. By the time they do, it'll be too late."

> **LESSON ONE: Do not act on unfounded expectations.**
>
> Isaac should not have sold his stock on unfounded expectations alone.

"Man, where did you come from?!" Ishmael asked because their views were often so disparate that he was sometimes embarrassed to call Isaac his twin.

"Twin, I can't help what other people will or won't do," Isaac continued, "I just decided that I don't have time for people to get excited about ACB, so I sold it all and bought some other stuff that I'll tell you about when we get together and compare our returns. What have you done, Malcolm, Martin, or is it Ché today?"

Ishmael, irritated by the implication that his left-wing political bent rendered him incapable of making good investment decisions, reminded Isaac of his impulsiveness. Isaac often had poor timing. "Very funny. Ha ha. Well, I guess you took a pretty big loss, because Dad bought those shares at $23.50. What did you sell them for?"

"Now Ishmael, don't worry about what I'm doing just yet. Worry about what you're doing."

"Well, I'm just sitting tight right now until I decide what I want to do. Plus, I think ACBN will go up again."

"Why?" Julene jumped in.

"I've been reading the papers, and I believe in what they're doing. And they've been profitable thus far. They don't have any real competitors from what I can see, so I'll just keep it for now," Ishmael said thoughtfully.

"Mom, what are you doing?" asked Isaac.

Julene was silent for a long time, then said, "I'm taking B.B.'s advice to mix it up a little. He said that I should never have all of my money in one company,

LESSON TWO: Do not refuse to sell just because you have an emotional attachment to an investment.

Ishmael clearly is not interested in building wealth right now. He has made assumptions about the quality of the investment based on "warm and fuzzy" feelings to provide an excuse for keeping the stock. He has an investment that will either appreciate, depreciate or both at varying periods of time.

and that I should sell some of the shares and reinvest in other companies, so that's what I'm doing."

"Which companies, Mom?" Isaac asked.

LESSON THREE: Do not invest without an adequate understanding.

Julene was right to take a professional's advice because she did not want to wait until she understood *everything* about investing before she started. However, even after you entrust your investments to a professional, seek to understand what you are invested in and why.

"Just like you told your brother, don't worry about what others are doing. Think about what you're doing and later, we'll see who did what," Julene snapped back.

Ishmael asked his mother whether she thought he should mix it up too, especially since B.B. thought it was too risky to be invested in just one company. She suggested that since his account was with Thomas, he should ask B.B. himself.

"I suspect that because I'm older, or because I'm less confident about what I'm doing, then I should rely on his advice more. I'm not sure."

"Well there's one thing I'm sure of," Isaac interjected, "it's that Ishmael and I should be doing about the same thing, given that we are the same age. Unless of course, Ishmael is afraid to take risks, or Ishmael is going to spend the money soon." Ishmael said nothing for he did not know what he planned to do.

"So the way it stands now, I have no ACBN, Ishmael is 100% in ACBN (wouldn't you know it), and, Mom, you've secretly mixed it up," concluded Isaac.

"All I know is that I want to make a lot of money," continued Isaac. "If I do well, Mom will give me more."

"So why do you want to make a lot of money? Can't you just make some money and be fine with that?" Ishmael asked.

"No, I want to make as much money as I can, and that means taking as much risk as I can by investing in a company or companies that have explosive growth potential. If I lose, then I lose," Isaac replied.

"Well, sons, I'm more interested in having earned *some* money. I'm looking forward to retirement, so any investment that's going to help me get there without blowing this money, that's what I'm interested in," Julene confirmed.

"Twin brother, what say you?" Isaac asked Ishmael.

"I'm not sure what my goals are yet, but I believe ACB

LESSON FOUR: Know your financial objectives before you buy or sell stock.

Julene, Ishmael and Isaac each owned ACB stock, but perhaps each had different financial priorities. Just because one person owns a particular stock doesn't mean you should too. Ask yourself the question, "What would I like my **net worth** to be in 5, 10, 25 and 50 years?" If owning the stock does not have the potential to appreciate in price enough to help you reach those quantified goals in the period of time set, you should not own it.

LESSON FIVE: Know the company best able and willing to capitalize on the exploitable business opportunity.

Ishmael did not know whether ACBN was really the company best suited to meet the entertainment needs of African-Americans. He was aware that there were major networks with "Black programming" and that there were African-Americans who watched TV regardless of the color of the actors. He did not ask whether the major networks posed a business threat to ACBN.

knows their business and will be profitable in the long-run," Ishmael replied.

"So, the race is on! I'll talk to y'all later, I have some investing to do." Isaac hung up first. As each of them hung up their phones they wondered whether they had made the right choices.

Julene Reads A Stock Page

Julene eventually made her way back to the welcoming and nurturing arms of the church. The love she received from its members was enough to encourage her that she belonged there, even in the absence of her husband (she often wondered what people would have thought of her had she not been married to The Reverend Marcus Jamison).

She entered Marcus's office for the first time since his death. She circled the wall, very slowly and ritualistically, just as she would have had Marcus been there. Just before she reached his desk, she stopped, looked up and around and imagined the oil portrait of Marcus that would soon grace the walls. She smiled with pride for the honor of her husband's legacy within the greater Mt. Zion AME legacy in Houston. When she reached his desk, she saw the newspaper he had been reading at the time of his death. Maybe she could determine what was on his mind at the time of his death. Nothing seemed unusual, until she noticed a check mark next to an article.

> *Houston Chronicle*, October 31 - ACBN, the ticker symbol for Ashanti Cable Broadcasting Network (ACB) Holdings, began trading on the New York Stock Exchange (NYSE). ACBN is the first Black-owned company to trade on the NYSE. Trading started at $17 per share and closed that day at $23 1/2 per share. 4.25 million shares representing 21% ownership in the company were offered to the public for sale. Donald Jackson, founder, chair, CEO and president, owns 56% of the shares. 400,000 shares were sold to individuals. The lead underwriter is First Maine Corporation.

Julene was intrigued, now that she knew more about what Marcus was thinking before he died. She found comfort in the thought that he wanted to be a part of something huge in terms of Black history. She wondered if the purchase of 400,000 shares by individuals like her husband was a lot, given that the president owned over two million shares. Clearly, thousands of people invested in a Black company, and that must be an indication that it is a good investment. Suddenly, she realized that she was reading a newspaper that was months old. What was news to her was now history. Did more people ever invest in ACB?

She stepped outside the church and walked across the street to the convenience store to get the latest Houston Chronicle. She turned to the business page, looked for the "Stocks" section and found ACBN under the symbols which were grouped alphabetically.

NEW YORK STOCK EXCHANGE COMPOSITE TRANSACTIONS										
				Quotations as of 4 p.m. Eastern Time April 9, 199-						
52 Weeks					Yld		Vol			Net
Hi	Lo	Stock	Sym	Div	%	PE	100s	Hi	Lo	Close	Chg
					-A-A-A-					
23.1	12³/₄	Ashanti	ACBN				439	14.375	14.125	14.25	

Julene found ACBN's high and low price for April 9th. The high was $14.375, the low was $14.125, and the closing was just between the high and low for the day at $14.25. So, Marcus's shares he bought at $23.50 were down $9.25 per share or about 40% less than he paid. She wondered who would buy stocks when the price was going down. She also wondered whether the individuals who purchased 400,000 shares on the first day still owned the stocks.

She looked at the column titled, "Volume 000's" that stated 439. What did that mean?

Just to get a sense of 52-week trading ranges and the number of shares traded, Julene looked throughout the stock pages for companies familiar to her. She saw that some companies had trading ranges of several dollars, with trading volumes in the hundreds of thousands. Comparing ACB to them, ACB did not garner as much investor interest as some of its competitors in entertainment.

Volume of sales (indicated by "100s" on a stock page) shows the total number of shares traded – both bought and sold – that day. The difference between the high and the low prices is the **trading range**. In this case there is a 52-week high/low and a daily high/low. If there is not that much difference in high and low prices, there may also be a lack of trading volume.

ACB Year 1 Events

B-Innovation Magazine, March – …Jackson was well on his way to becoming Wall Street's latest entrepreneur celebré. Then came the conference call between Jackson and stock analysts on the afternoon of December 16. The analysts' question was simple: Was viewership eroding? No, said Jackson. The analysts asked, why did ACB report reaching fewer viewers than Barnaby Viewcast Co. (the television-audience research firm) counted? It took Jackson several days to clarify the discrepancy (ACB counted only paid subscribers to the cable network while Barnaby's number included new subscribers enjoying temporary free service).

Meanwhile, shareholders began selling. The stock's price plunged to $15 a share…"It was just a question of newness to the marketplace and our inexperience, initially, in answering the kinds of questions they were phrasing," says Jackson…First Maine equity research analyst Mary Borland forecasts that 'over the next three to five years, [ACB's] revenues should grow in excess of 20% annually, operating cash flows 30% and earnings 40%.' She says this will be largely the result of scheduled increases in cable operating fees, more new subscribers due to operators upgrading channel capacity, increased advertiser focus on reaching the black consumer market and the company's low cost structure."

The Street Reports, April 3 – ACB Holdings reported sales of $35.8 million, had 31 million subscribers, and Robert L. Jackson owned 56% of the voting shares. 9,800 shares were traded that day. Close at $14.75

The Street Reports, May 12 – George Feldon of IS Financial Services, reiterates that investors should buy ACBN. 6,100 shares were traded that day. Close at $15.25.

The Street Reports, June 12 – ACB Holdings reported a 40% rise in net income on 22% revenue growth for the fiscal third quarter due to increases in cable advertising and subscriber revenue. ACB had 29.5 million subscribers. Revenue rose to $16 million from $13.1 million. ACB anticipated losses related to its magazines until the magazines became fully established 3,100 shares were traded that day. Close at $14.875

The D.C. Courier, October 22 – ACB mentioned in its annual earnings statement, there was an internal investigation into financial irregularities amounting to about $700,000. According to ACB, some unauthorized payments were made by corporate officials for goods and services that weren't received...The company also announced that the former chief financial officer and comptroller left the company. $700,000 was equal to nearly 6% of the company's total annual profit and 23 percent of its profit during the fourth quarter. 1,400 shares were traded. Closed at $13.125.

The Street Reports, December 9 – ACB Holdings, Inc. reported a slight increase in net income on higher revenue for its fiscal first quarter, largely attributable to gains in programming fees and ad revenue. Volume was 59300, at closed at $14.875.

The Street Reports, December 12 – ACB reported a slight increase in net income on higher revenue for its fiscal first quarter, largely attributable to gains in programming fees and ad revenue. 600 shares were traded on December 14th, the next trading day. Closed at $14.50.

Year 2

*Keep competition in perspective. It can diminish
your humanity and improve your abilities.*

Lessons Learned in the First Year of Investing

"Oh, no!" Ishmael was shocked and angry. Not because his
stock was still down from when his father bought it, but because
few people were trading ACBN. He began to think about what

NEW YORK STOCK EXCHANGE COMPOSITE TRANSACTIONS										
				Quotations as of 4 p.m. Eastern Time February 9, 199-						
52 Weeks					Yld		Vol			Net
Hi	Lo	Stock	Sym	Div	%	PE	100s	Hi	Lo	Close	Chg
					-A-A-A-						
32	23³/₁₆	Ashanti	ACBN				215	17.375	17	17.25	

Isaac said a year ago: that Black folks do not invest in stocks.
But what about the other people? Didn't they see the potential in
ACBN? Or did they not even know about ACBN?

After some thought, Ishmael could not imagine why they
would know it. ACB did not air shows like the other TV stations
– mainly, there were only Black people on ACB's shows. Maybe
he should have sold his stock, but selling it was like selling-out his
people. To his way of thinking, "How can a Black-owned com-

pany serve the needs of the Black community without Black support?" He concluded that it was not possible. Ishmael reasoned that ACB had only been public just over a year, and that it would take time before people, Black and White, became interested in the stock. In the meantime, he would hold on to it.

Ishmael picked up the phone to call his mother and twin. This was the moment for which they had waited a year: the time to compare their investment results. Ishmael steadied his hand, and firmed up his rationale for keeping ACBN, knowing that Isaac would probably be the winner, and therefore more deserving of the money his mother promised. He dialed Julene's number, then Isaac.

"Twin brother, I've got some good news and some bad news. Is Mom on the phone?"

"Hi, Sweetheart. How are you?"

Isaac loved being called Sweetheart, for on occasion, he needed confirmation that he was his mother's favorite son.

"I'm fine, except I still don't have an offer, at least not yet. Lots of interviews, but no real offers, yet." He asked his mother about her health, asked Ishmael about his new job, shared information about his temporary receptionist job, then said, "Hey, let's get down to it, I have some more investing to do!"

Whenever Isaac said this, it would annoy Ishmael because Isaac liked to leave the impression that he was always busy with some type of business transaction.

"I'll start," Ishmael said. "I have less than what I started with. End of story."

Julene asked if he still owned ACBN, and only ACBN. Ishmael confirmed that he did, and why.

"Believe it or not, I've started looking at *The Street Reports* when a copy is in the coffee shop, and I read that they're making money."

"ACB is making money, and you aren't. Isn't that ironic?" Isaac jabbed.

Julene asked if Isaac was doing any better.

"Well Mom, twin," started Isaac in his booming business voice, "I have more or less than what I started with. I sold ACBN at a major loss back when it was $14, so I lost $2,014 and add $30 for the cost of the trade, and I only had $1,984 to reinvest. So, I split it up three ways. I didn't want all my money in one company.

"With the proceeds of the sale, I bought 2,868 shares of Chipps for about 22 cents per share, 106 shares of PCinabox, Inc. for $5.93 per share, and 110 shares of iHear.net for $5.718 per share. It cost me $90 to place those three trades, so my balance right now is less than what I started with. If they don't begin to go up in about a month, I'm going to have to sell them."

"Why are you giving them only a month?" asked Ishmael.

"Twin, I don't want to be an old man before I become wealthy. The sooner, the better," stated Isaac with less confidence than he projected.

Julene had never heard of the companies Isaac had chosen. She worried that he would blow his father's money on hair-brained notions of a science fiction-like existence where all human communications and human interactions are devalued.

"Sweetheart, why did you choose those companies?" Julene asked. "I would have looked at some older, bigger companies that you know will be around a long time."

LESSON SIX: Diversify your investments across companies and industries.

Isaac was right to spread his investments in a number of companies, but each company is in the same broadly defined industry called high technology. One is a microchip manufacturer, one is a computer manufacturer that relies on microchips to work, and the other is a communications medium that requires a computer that relies on a microchip. His portfolio is underdiversified as it relates to industries. He risks losses if the industry he chose falls out of favor with investors. On the other hand, if the market perceives high technology as the industry with the most growth potential, the reward potential is high.

Isaac responded that he was not concerned about losing the money, even if it was his father's because he knew that his father would want him to take some calculated risks. "Dad used to say that the problem with Black folks is that we don't want to take risks with our money, that's why we never have any."

Ishmael thought affectionately about his father, and for a moment was saddened by memories of an embittered corporate middle manager.

"Isaac, I'm not trying to be funny or anything, but I have a question for you. You've been looking for a decent job for several months now. Why do you think you haven't been offered a position?"

Isaac wondered where Ishmael was going with the question.

"What I'm getting at," Ishmael continued, "is why are you investing in companies that aren't hiring you, and probably aren't hiring a whole lot of Black folks? Haven't you heard of the phrase "racial ravine?" I think Dad invested in ACB because it was about investing Black, and now you've sold all your shares, and invested that money in White-owned, white-managed companies.

I don't get that."

Isaac was stunned because he had not given any thought to the color of the CEO, nor the color of the employees. He had wondered on occasion why it was taking a long time to get a job, but he reasoned that great jobs are not easy to find.

"Mom said she wanted us to learn how to invest. Period. I guess you think that because you've got a job as a social worker, then that makes you better than me? Well twin, I have news for you. *Anybody* can be a social worker – I don't even know why you went to college for that, they would have paid you what you're making right now with just a G.E.D. And guess what? You were probably the only brother in Houston who applied for the job, making you an unopposed candidate!

"Isaac, that wasn't necessary!" Julene said.

"He started it!" Ishmael, now embarrassed, caught himself reacting to his twin as if they were still boys.

"Well, I guess that's my clue to sign off. I'll talk to y'all later." Ishmael hung up the phone, but his mother and brother remained on the phone.

Ishmael looked around his studio apartment; he focused on his rock-hard futon, then his so-called desk and wondered if Isaac was right. He wondered whether he had taken his father's advice too seriously – to give to the needy without regard for much compensation. He figured that a time would come when he wanted more out of life, not more in the way of living, but perhaps more in the way of material things. He imagined marriage and later a son who looked just like his father. They would name him little Marc. But would he be able to send little Marc to college like big Marc

A Lesson in Creating a Discipline Around Selling:
How to nurture an uninformed, shortsighted, greedy and impatient mind.

1. If the fundamental nature (leadership, products, services, functions, labor, etc.) of the company hasn't changed since you bought it, don't sell. If you do not know the fundamental nature of the company, investigate.

2. Has the economy changed to such an extent that it will have a negative impact on the company's operations or the industry as a whole? If it hasn't, don't sell. If you do not know the state of the economy, know it.

3. If the company has performed consistently with analysts' expectations, do not sell. If you do not know who the analysts are, and if you do not know whether the analysts know what they're talking about, investigate. *Institutional Investor* and the *Wall Street Journal* rank analysts. These publications will give you an indication of how analysts rate against their peers. Also, read the business pages to see who's quoted often, and evaluate whether their opinions are "on the mark." You must also determine whether an analyst's comments are influenced by his or her relationship with the company being rated. A less than positive rating may result in lack of future access to corporate executives.

4. If the stock price has not appreciated consistently with the analyst's estimates, do not sell based on that alone. Determine the reason for the failure. It may have less to do with the company, and more to do with the company's competitors, views on the economy, and even positive opinions about the company (the stock price has risen a lot and quickly, and investors sell some shares for short-term profits.)

5. If you do not know the technical forecast for the stock, do not sell.

Creating a Sell Discipline Cont'd

6. Just because the stock has reached your expected price point doesn't mean it won't go higher. Do not sell if you do not know if there is greater appreciation, and the time frame for that appreciation.

7. If you do not know whether the economy and/or the fundamental nature of the company have affected the risk vs. the reward profile, do not sell.

8. From a valuation standpoint (price of the stock in relationship to the corporate earnings), is the stock price attractive or perceived by others as potentially attractive? If so, don't sell it.

9. Determine what would negatively affect (in the mind of the public) the reputation of a company. If there is potential for rumors, gossip, or news about corporate personalities, product defects, poor employee relations, anti-competitive practices that could negatively affect the price of the stock, read the newspapers and keep your eyes and ears open for information. If there is no information negatively affecting the company's reputation in the mind of the public, do not sell.

10. When your financial needs and goals change, evaluate whether your current investments have the potential to meet your goals. If your needs and goals haven't changed, do not sell.

---

had sent him and Isaac? Now was not the time to fret over money. Now was the time to help people.

Julene scolded Isaac, "I want you to call your brother right now and apologize to him."

Isaac called his twin and Ishmael accepted his apology. They had never been angry with each other for more than an hour.

"Okay Mom, it's time for you to spill the beans. You're working with Mr. Freeman and…" Isaac began to laugh, "What did he advise you to do, and more importantly, do you still have any money?" The twins began to laugh uproariously.

Julene was amused and she could not blame her sons for making fun of B.B. because he was strange. "Well sons, I have some money, actually more than what I started with. I'll let you in on a little secret, but I'm not going to tell you how much I made because the contest for additional cash is between you two, not me. All I can tell you is that B.B. put me in a diversified portfolio. He said that the first thing to do is determine if the economy is strong and going to remain strong. Then you should look at the variety of industries and companies within those industries, and choose the stocks accordingly.

LESSON SEVEN: Create your own strategy for diversifying your stock portfolio.

Julene, who chose to use professional investment advice, decided to own several stocks in companies from a variety of industries. There are two overall strategies for creating a diversified portfolio – top-down or bottom-up.
1) The top-down strategy is when the investor first looks at trends in the general economy, and then selects industries, and then companies that should benefit from those trends.
2) The bottom-up strategy is when the investor looks at the performance of the company first. The belief is that no matter the state of the economy, these companies will perform well.

Julene explained, "ACBN is in the entertainment business, and therefore part of the Consumer Cyclical group."

Size Diversification

There are three primary size categories to diversification – small, mid-, and large capitalization (caps) companies. The size of the company theoretically allows the investor to speculate on the room for growth (i.e., a small cap company can potentially grow more than a large cap company that already has significant market share. There are two ways to determine the size of the company, by ranking and by actual capitalization. For example, Morningstar (a company that rates mutual funds), states that the largest 1% of U.S. companies are considered "Giants", the next 4%, Large, the next 15% Medium, the next 30% Small, and the bottom 50% Micro.

Price Styles

There are two primary "price" styles – value and growth. Both are expected to appreciate, but at different rates.

1) **Value** means the stock price is low relative to corporate earnings, perhaps because the company is not in an exciting business segment, perhaps because of a pending lawsuit or another negative reason. Buying the stock today does not give the investor any reason to think the price will appreciate significantly in a short period of time.
2) **Growth** in this context means no matter the stock price today, and no matter the corporate earnings, the price is expected to appreciate because it is a popular stock to own.

The diversified portfolio can be constructed from the top down or bottom up, and consist of a variety of sizes, or similar sizes, purchased at a value, with short-term growth in mind, or a combination thereof. Investors should chose a diversification strategy based on what they expect will allow them to meet their financial goals with the least amount of risk.

"What's that?" the twins asked in unison.

"I'm not sure how to explain it technically, but it's probably any company whose product sales are affected by economic cycles. People buy more or less of it depending on whether the economy is strong or weak. B.B. told me that Consumer Cyclicals include businesses in clothing, restaurants, casinos, and cars – things like that, and entertainment."

LESSON EIGHT: Know the industry groups.

The industry groups include: Basic & Raw Materials, Capital Goods, Conglomerates, Consumer Cyclicals, Consumer Non-Cyclicals, Energy, Financial, Healthcare, Industrial, Technology, Telecommunications, Transportation, and Utilities. Certain industries tend to experience more growth or more stagnation or loss depending on the economic cycle. Consequently, Julene, Isaac and Ishmael will have a greater chance of investing successfully if they know the industry groups poised to do well in the current economic cycle.

"Mom," Ishmael began to worry, "did Mr. Freeman tell you whether ACB would suffer in a bad economy? The way I see it, watching ACB is not like going to movie. It doesn't cost much, and when the economy is bad, people might stay home more and watch TV because it's cheap entertainment."

"Twin," Isaac could not help but share his opinion, "I think the economy is the least of your problems. The question is, even in good economic times, will people invest in ACB? I say the answer is no. Furthermore, look at it this way. Have you ever thought about the state of the economy before buying a movie ticket? Probably not. And if you haven't, how many other people haven't. No. You've got bigger problems than the economy."

Julene, finally able to get a word in edgewise, answered that her meeting with B.B. was very interesting as always…

Terrell Freeman was about to make the biggest decision of his life. He would either stay and help his father Thomas continue in his business, or he would, like many of his friends, go North. It was in the North that a Negro could stand tall, be a man, provide for his family with a good paying job, buy a home without the discrimination and downright persecution you would face in the South, and find a sophisticated Negro woman, dressed in fine things and unencumbered by all that "ole time" religion that the Southern women were brought up with.

Though, there were a few downsides – Terrell would miss his family terribly, he would need a job and new friends, and he would be cold in the winter – the decision was made. The downsides were merely minor inconveniences, challenges actually. Terrell asked Thomas' permission to move North, and Thomas reluctantly granted his son that wish, asking that Terrell return home when things got too tough. He could have his old job, and inherit the business upon his passing. Terrell, grateful for his father's love and generosity, packed his bags and left.

It was cold all right. Much to his surprise, the women seemed as cold as the wind, but he made it North. With the help of friends, he got a job in a factory paying a lot more than he made in his father's business. After a few months, he had enough money to get a room in a tenement. He looked all over town, but for some reason or another, he could not rent in many places. He hoped it had nothing to do with the fact that he was a Negro, since the North was supposed to be different than the South. He finally settled in an apartment in his friend's building (just as nice as the other buildings, just all Negro), and got into the routine of going to the factory at the same time every workday, and leaving at the same time, every workday. He found the work monotonous, but did not tell his father.

One day Terrell overheard two of his white co-workers talking about their pay, and he began to wonder why they were paid more for doing exactly the same job (maybe it was because they had been there longer). When he discovered that whites were paid more than Negroes, Terrell became in-censed, and he approached other Negro employees about the matter. The following week, Terrell became one of the founding members of the Negro's Union for Parity.

"Mom, has Mr. Freeman taught you anything about money?" Ishmael was irritated, mostly because his mother seemed to be learning nothing from her advisor, but also because of his own fear and insecurity about keeping ACBN. As he remembered his father's desire to invest in a Black-owned company serving the Black community, the thought soothed him.

"Twin, let me ask you a question. Do you know of any other company that is recognized by millions of Black folks, and is pub-licly owned?" Isaac asked

"Well I'm just going to hang onto this stock until ACB goes

bankrupt or goes out of business, or has some big competitor, or…"

"Until you learn how to invest, Brother X," Isaac joked. "Mom, did Mr. Freeman advise you to sell all of your ACBN shares?"

Julene sensed that Isaac was fishing for expert advice, though he did not want to admit that B.B.'s opinion might be worth something to him. "I kept some shares, but this isn't about me, it's about you two and who has invested well. Isaac, your account may be worth more than Ishmael's, but I don't get the sense you know any more about investing than Ishmael does. Ishmael you've held onto ACBN, but you didn't give me a good reason why you did so. Y'all didn't even know what Consumer Cyclicals meant. This time next year be better prepared to earn this money. I'm going to keep it for myself, for now."

"But Mom," the twins said in unison.

"But nothing – you two are lazy, and I won't reward laziness. I'm going to get off this phone now. We'll talk later."

Isaac was shocked that with all his trading experience and success, his mother would see him as a failure. "Well at least Ishmael is impressed!" he thought.

Ishmael thought the whole "contest" was bizarre, and that the money his father left his mother had changed her. Money was suddenly this all-important element in her life. "She never once talked about investing while Dad was alive," he thought. Her little contest proved just how strange his family was, especially his twin.

Making Life Choices

Ishmael chose to work as a counselor in a drug rehabilitation center. His life's mission was to show compassion toward the needy. Grandpa would say that helping the needy would stop you from being greedy, "There ain't no fun in being needy, but the Devil will get 'cha if you're greedy." Ishmael no longer wondered why he was so different than his twin.

His salary was enough for a studio apartment. Yet, he had to make the choice between deferring his school loans and buying a car. He chose to begin paying his loans. Luckily, his job did not require him to wear business attire – blue jeans and a shirt with a collar were fine. His worldly belongings included a new futon without the frame; a desk he made with two file cabinets and an unfinished door; a lamp from the Salvation Army; and the stereo his parents bought him when he made the Dean's List his first semester in college. Overall, he was not doing badly.

Ishmael and Isaac grew up having practically everything they needed. The Jamisons moved to a good school district so that their sons would be prepared for college. They had new clothes every school year; they excelled in scholastics and sports – Ishmael football, and Isaac soccer (it was more cosmopolitan). As a result, Isaac went to Abbington College on a partial soccer scholarship. His parents were somewhat disappointed that he chose Abbington over a historically Black college, but they understood his reasoning – to succeed in an integrated world, he had to step outside his comfort zone early.

Ishmael chose State University majoring in social work. He and Isaac agonized together where they would go to school and Isaac insisted that Ishmael go to Abbington.

"Look, we have never lived apart from each other, first. Second, Abbington College offers so much more than State. It has a reputation throughout the nation as a place where brilliant people are educated. Third, you get to know future business leaders. Fourth, they probably offer some classes in social work so that you will be able to learn what you want to learn." But Isaac could not convince Ishmael that Abbington was a place where he would feel comfortable.

"Yeah, yeah, but I really don't see how knowing a future business leader is going to help me counsel folks. Plus, I think I'll just have a better time at S.U., if you know what I mean." He often referred to meeting young women as 'you know what I mean'."

Whenever Isaac could not convince Ishmael to do something, he would quote from the Marcus Jamison book of life, "Remember what Dad used to say? He'd say, 'You're not going to climb the ladder to success unless you: a) hang out with those who will; b) suck up to those who will; and c) work hard and hope those you suck up to will remember and promote you. Then you have to start all over for the next promotion.' Do you think Dad was wrong?"

Marcus Jamison believed in building your own ladder simply because the world expected that Blacks worked for others. In his view that phenomenon had persisted far too long. Ishmael never fully understood his father's anger, nor did Isaac. Their memories, though, served to ground them. In time, they would come to understand fully what their father had experienced.

ACB Year 2 Events

B-Innovation Magazine, January – "Donald Jackson…is leading a partnership to acquire Cloud Top Cablevision, a Denver-based cable system. Arrow-Mitchell Cable signed a letter of intent to sell its 42.5% stake in Cloud Top to Jackson in September. The holders of the remaining 57.7% stake in Cloud Top are expected to sell to Jackson's group shortly after the Arrow-Mitchell deal is approved."

March 4 – Close $16.375, High $16.375, Low $16.00, Volume 20100

March 5 – ACB said net income for the fiscal second climbed to $3.3 million, or 16 cents a share, from $2.9 million, or 14 cents a share, a year earlier. Revenue climbed 20% to $18 million from $15 million, bolstered by a 20% gain in advertising and subscriber revenue. Net for the six months climbed 19% to $6.2 million, or 30 cents a share, from $5.2 million, or 26 cents a share, a year earlier. Revenue for the period rose 26% to $35.4 million from $28.2 million, as advertising revenue climbed 24% and subscriber revenue rose 26%. High $16.25, Low $16.25, Close $16.25 Volume 200.

Corporate profits are not necessarily the same as return on your investment. Return on your investment includes dividends and a higher market price per share of stock. Look for acceptable corporate profits year after year, even if the share price has not increased – there may be an objective reason for future investor interest.

The Street Reports, March 11 – ACB's board authorizes a plan to repurchase up to 650,000 of its Class A shares in the open market because it believes the stock is undervalued. There were about 12.7 million Class A shares outstanding.

B-Innovation Magazine, September 22 – Jackson says the acquisition of Active Viewer Pays allows his company to reach three primary goals: to increase distribution in urban locations; to enhance ad sales through cross-channel promotions; and to create the first vehicle to distribute films targeted to black audiences. He also says the service, renamed ACB Action Theatre, placed him in a market exhibiting strong growth.

September 23 – ACB Holdings Corp announces the launch of a separate all-jazz programming network in the fall of next year.

December 16 – 31% gain in fiscal first-quarter net income due to advertising revenue increase and increase in cable subscribers. ACB said losses in its magazine operations narrowed to $832,000 from $907,000 a year ago.

The Street Reports, December 16 – Net for the quarter ending October 31st rose to $3.8 million or 18 cents a share form $2.9 million or 14 cents a share a year earlier. Advertising revenue rose 32%, subscriber revenue 22%. Total revenue rose 37% for the core cable business rose to $23.7 million.

December 22 – ACB announced that it will join Video Rental Entertainment Corp. to produce family-oriented films aimed at African-American audiences, called ACB Pictures, initially expects to finance three or four films in the $1.5 to $3 million range through independent production companies. ACB shares rose 37.5 cents to $18.375 and Video Rental slipped 50 cents to close at $30.375.

Joint ventures are not always perceived as positive moves for both companies.

Year 3

Rise to the intellectual challenge or fall deeper into ignorant splendor.

Isaac Finds His Calling

After several months of interviewing and hob-nobbing at Abbington College alumni gatherings in Houston, Isaac Jamison networked his way into an entry-level position at Continental Bank. He maintained friendly business relationships between Continental and its customers. Just a year and a half into his customer relations position, his biggest decisions boiled down to which customers would he phone monthly, quarterly or yearly.

Isaac was happy to be employed in a place where he could wear a suit, meet new people, and be where he often said he wanted to be – where the money is. Yet, he was also disappointed that he was not doing something more intellectually challenging. While it was not easy dealing with difficult people, by and large, his charm was often more important than his intellect. Therefore, he spent his time thinking of other things he could do, like working in Continental's Capital Asset Management division (CCAM). It was in CCAM that he thought he could make the most money. He had heard of the hundreds of millions of dollars invested with CCAM, and thought that if he could only get a "piece of that," he would be on easy street. First, he would be a broker, then a manager, then a regional manager, then a divisional manager, then a high-level executive in headquarters, then the CEO. It was on days like today that he would daydream about his climb up the corporate ladder.

On this day an unfamiliar woman walked into the bank. Strange women walked into the bank all of the time, but this woman was different somehow. She was younger than most of their regular bank customers. Dressed in a blue and white pinstriped suit, she was effortlessly and flawlessly beautiful – no special hairstyle, hardly any make-up, if any. Unlike most people her skin seemed to glisten underneath the bank's artificial light. She walked as if she was there on a mission. What could it have been? She must not have had an account with the bank, otherwise he would have known her, or maybe she was a long-time customer whom he had not yet met. Isaac thought that today was his lucky day. In his mind, he would approach her like he was the manager of the bank and not just the customer relations guy.

As she walked toward Isaac, he reached for her hand and said, "Hello, I'm Isaac Jamison with Continental Bank. May I assist you this morning?"

She replied that she had an appointment with CCAM to discuss her account. "Oh my God, the sister is rich!" Isaac thought to himself. He broke into a wide smile, and paused to think of how he could get to know her without being unprofessional and risking what might already be a great business relationship between her and CCAM.

His smile began to melt down her business purpose and it was just at the time her eyes met his, he said, "Again, I'm Isaac Jamison, and I'm responsible for making sure our customers are satisfied. Are you satisfied, Mrs…?" Isaac paused to see if she understood that he really wanted to know if she had a husband, and if so, if she was happy with him because he couldn't see her with anyone but him.

"*Ms*. Perkins. Gloria." Isaac knew they were on the same page. "I guess you're the person I should be talking to. I'm interested in having my portfolio evaluated and I'm looking for a new money manager. I'm not satisfied with the level of service I've received, and I want to know if Continental Bank's Capital Asset Management service is what I'm looking for."

Isaac was in love, but he was not sure if it was the woman or the money he loved the most. "Ms. Perkins, I'm happy to take a brief look at your portfolio and give you a preliminary evaluation. If you have a few minutes, I'd like to ask you a few questions, then tell you what CCAM has to offer. Would you like to have a seat at my desk?"

She was eager to hear what he had to say, though Isaac appeared a lot younger than other investment professionals with whom she had met. Gloria removed statements from a manila folder marked "Stock Portfolio, 3rd Quarter" and handed them to Isaac. Isaac had never seen a stock portfolio except his own, and did not know what he would say about hers. Nevertheless, he wanted so much to know more about her, and her money, that he was willing to risk saying the wrong thing and risk losing his job.

He stared at the statement, looked at Gloria, looked at the statement again, made some notes on his notepad, looked at the statement again, and began to draw a diagram. He handed his notepad to Gloria and asked her if she knew what it was. Isaac informed her that it was a cotton plant.

"Are you a student of B.B. Freeman?" she asked in pleasant surprise.

Hearing the tone in her voice, and wanting to impress her, he said, "I've always admired Mr. Freeman's pedagogy in the area of technical analysis."

Gloria explained that she was already familiar with technical analysis, and what she really needed was someone to manage her portfolio on an ongoing basis. Isaac wondered why she had not taken her account to Freeman, but reminded himself that as eccentric as Freeman was, he would not want his account there either. Trying to think quickly, as a student of Mr. Freeman's what else would he say to her about her account? He remembered he had not stayed in Freeman's office long enough to get the gist of his story, but if Freeman had an approach, perhaps he could successfully borrow the approach for a moment.

Gloria looked at Isaac and noticed some tension in his face and hands. He seemed young, and she knew that he was not a broker because brokers at asset management companies did not sit at open desks on the main floor of the bank. She thought he was physically attractive, but more importantly, he seemed ambitious, and a man with ambition attracted her.

"Mr. Jamison. I don't have a lot of time right now, but I'd like to meet with you next week. I'll leave this with you for now and come back on Thursday at 3:00 p.m. If you have an hour then, I'd like to get your opinion."

Isaac checked his blank calendar, "Ms. Perkins, please come back Thursday at 3:15 and we'll discuss your portfolio at that time."

Gloria left, and Isaac was relieved. He might not be able to think as quick on his feet, but he would know what to say next week when she returned. Isaac could not wait to go home to call his twin about Gloria. If Gloria was not married (her statement was only in her name), he was sure he had a chance to go out with her, especially if he impressed her with his investment knowledge.

"What knowledge!?" he asked himself. He took Gloria's file home with him to begin studying and preparing for his next meeting with her. If only she had given him two weeks…

Buy and Sell Orders

Later that evening at his apartment, Isaac pulled out his last investment statement and reviewed it. With what little he had to work with, he doubted whether he could "pull it off" with Gloria. He had just three stocks, and Gloria had twenty-three – with a total value of about $837,000.

He had never researched a company before, so he could not really tell her about each company, their businesses, their competitors, their history, or their market positions for short-term and long-term growth.

Isaac knew he could not pull together a fundamental

LESSON NINE: Determine what professional analysts say about your stocks or the stocks you're interested in buying.

An analyst works with a brokerage house, bank, or mutual fund, and studies the business practices, products, and markets of companies. They then make recommendations on whether investors should buy, sell, or hold stock. *The Wall Street Journal* and *Institutional Investor* rank analysts by the accuracy of their estimates.

Dolphin Asset Management
Quarterly Review

Gloria Perkins
1234 Juice Road
Houston, TX 45634
Acct. #678-96-33 B

Sam Supperhaim
713-333-2345

	Date Purchased	# of Shares	Purchase Price	Symbol	Principal	Qtr. Close	Current Value
1.	3/31/91	15	23	ABD	$345	26	$390
2.	3/31/91	500	15	ACC	$7,500	13	$6,500
3.	3/31/91	300	20	BXY	$6,000	53	$15,900
4.	3/31/91	600	47	BZT	$28,200	48	$28,800
5.	4/3/91	1,250	150	BZZ	$187,500	213	$266,250
6.	4/3/91	200	73	CACT	$14,600	95	$19,000
7.	4/14/91	35	6	CDRM	$210	25	$875
8.	4/14/91	300	211	CFV	$63,300	191	$57,300
9.	5/2/91	300	106	DABE	$31,800	73	$21,900
10.	5/26/91	1,400	87	DBV	$121,800	92	$128,800
11.	6/14/91	2,000	4	DCC	$8,000	12	$24,000
12.	8/3/91	150	213	EVV	$31,950	185	$27,750
13.	2/5/92	300	14	FDKO	$4,200	3	$900
14.	2/5/92	600	76	GKKM	$45,600	82	$49,200
15.	5/8/92	3,500	29	GMN	$101,500	40	$140,000
16.	6/28/92	300	22	HGJ	$6,600	15	$4,500
17.	6/28/92	100	79	HTRW	$7,900	56	$5,600
18.	7/8/92	71	167	IQW	$11,857	164	$11,644
19.	7/8/92	20	65	IZIP	$1,300	72	$1,440
20.	7/8/92	45	52	J	$2,340	87	$3,915
21.	1/23/93	750	10	LKM	$7,500	8	$6,000
22.	1/23/93	80	211	KLP	$16,880	167	$13,360
23.	1/23/93	200	33	Y	$6,600	14	$2,800

analysis on each company. He would just accept that he was ignorant in the area. As gifted with gab as he was known to be, he did not want to risk exposure with Gloria, an experienced investor, and a most beautiful woman. Yet, Ms. Loaded and Beautiful expected him to provide her with some investment advice. The thought of deriving a strategy on when to sell, buy, or hold any of these 23 stocks overwhelmed him. How would he know which orders to place? Maybe he would just tell her to hold on to each of them until she needed to sell shares for cash. Yeah, that was what he would do. Or he could call B.B. Freeman and get a quick lesson in portfolio management.

He picked up the phone to dial Freeman, hoping he was not there and that Freeman could just return the call with an answer and no off-the-wall stories.

"This is B.B. Freeman."

Surprised into speechlessness, Isaac sputtered, "This is Isaac Jamison. You're my mother's broker, you may remember meeting me."

B.B. was silent for a moment. "Yes, I remember. What can I do for you?"

Isaac was surprised that Freeman did not give him a hard time. He proceeded to tell Freeman the purpose of his call and Freeman asked if Isaac knew about Tyrone Freeman–

Tyrone Freeman was Tobi's great grandson. He looked a lot like Tobi, tall and burly. Tyrone did not like what he had seen in the North – he found it quite brutal. Not that the South was any better. He had heard from others that there was only one way a Negro could have a nice lifestyle that was also free of racial prejudice, in the U.S. armed services. His father Terrell begged Tyrone not to fight for the U.S. because it was not his country to fight for, and the so-called enemy had done nothing to the Negro. Tyrone was determined. Who could blame him? His great grandfather had been a slave in the South, his father a sharecropper in the South, and his father an exploited factory worker in the North. Why not get into the Army and serve in Europe, he thought? It did not matter that there were Negro-only platoons – all he wanted was to get out of the United States and be the first man in his family to be treated with dignity.

"Ugh!" Isaac said after he hung-up the phone. It was bad judgment to think Freeman could have helped. Then again, his mother was happy with her relationship with Freeman. Maybe he could simply refer Gloria to Thomas Securities rather than CCAM and give a brother like Freeman a break. But how would he benefit if she took her money somewhere else? I sure wish I could be her advisor, he thought.

Isaac began to wonder how long he would continue to feel "out of the game," and how long it would take before he could get

LESSON TEN: Invest with as much information as you can gather and understand.

Isaac was unwilling to delve into the news and financial reports because doing so meant that he might miss out on immediate appreciation opportunities in the stock market. Yet, he realized that he was taking more risk than necessary by investing without information. What he was willing to do with his money was not a prudent approach for dealing with other people's money. Treat your investment dollars as if that money belonged to a loved one. Ask questions and seek out information.

into the game. With new resolve, he grabbed his investment file again and asked himself why he chose the stocks he did.

He hoped that Gloria's portfolio was based on something more objective than his "this is a popular stock today" strategy. But the bottom line is the money, and effective trading will get you more in the short-term if you do it the right way, he thought. To do it the right way though, he had to be a great market timer.

LESSON ELEVEN: Determine your objective: to be a stock trader or a better investor.

Most people who invest in the market are working jobs while the market is open. If you are working full-time while trading stocks, something important will not get done. Either your market timing will be off, or your job performance will suffer because you are concentrating on your investments.

Isaac returned his attention to his statement, focusing on the lack of upward movement in his three stocks. He had had enough. His patience was wearing thin because he had been told that these companies were going to "take off" and that he would make a lot of money. After a few years of being an investor, it was time that he began to better anticipate the up-turns and downturns in his investments.

Isaac knew how to place a **Market Order** to buy or sell a stock. Market orders meant that the order would be ex-

LESSON TWELVE: Invest with changing market conditions in mind.

If your stocks are not meeting your expectations and do not have the potential to meet your expectations in the time frame you have set for reaching your goals, re-evaluate not only the fundamental trends, but your tolerance for risk. It may be that holding onto the stock is inconsistent with your growth, income or growth and income objective.

ecuted at that current market price. It is the only order that is guaranteed to be executed. But tonight, Isaac was not interested in guaranteed executions, he wanted to "play the market," as it were.

That evening he decided he would place an **At-the-opening** order to sell each of his slumping stocks, so that his order would be executed when the market opened the next day. But should he simply place a market order to sell at-the-opening not knowing the pricing trend for the next day? He referred to the closing prices on his stocks to determine what the selling price at the opening would probably be.

Isaac was not sure he wanted to sell all his stocks. He was interested in limiting additional losses, but wanted to take advantage of gains if his stocks had a good day. He decided to place a sell **Limit Order** on all three stocks, meaning the stocks would be sold if the prices fell below certain prices. He did not have in mind a stock he wanted to purchase at a certain price, therefore he decided not to enter a buy limit order to buy at a maximum price or better.

"Playing the market" could be fun, he thought. Considering his investments more deeply, he thought maybe each stock would not necessarily go in the same direction. Maybe one of his stocks would go higher in price than the day before. He wanted to be sure that the stock was sold once it hit a certain price. It was also possible that his stock would lower in price from the day before. If it did, he wanted to limit his losses. Either way, he wanted to profit *and* cut his losses.

He placed two **Stop Orders**, one a **buy stop** (he might as well buy some stock while he was at it), the other a **sell stop**, both **Good-till-canceled** (though he could have placed them as day orders or any other time-limit orders). That way, he would not have to re-enter the orders every day.

Isaac knew that in placing these types of orders that the orders might be executed during the day because of market movements. Even though a price can go up and down many times during the day, he was willing to risk losing additional price appreciation if the stocks went beyond the stop prices. He decided that he would cancel his orders if they were not executed in a week.

Isaac realized that he had so many choices, but very little money to "play" with. He imagined that he was managing Gloria's nearly $1,000,000 portfolio and all he could do with it. Yet, he began to tire of all the types of orders; trying to match them with 23 stocks was just too much for one night.

A **stop order** to buy the stock is set above the current market price and is usually used to protect a profit or to limit a loss on a short sale (the sale of a stock not owned by the seller). When the stock price reaches the stop price (the specific price the stock has traded at), the order would be executed. A stop order to sell is set at a price below the current market price and is used to protect a profit or limit a loss on a stock already purchased at a higher price.

LESSON THIRTEEN: Mutual funds may provide an appropriate alternative to a self-directed and excessively traded stock portfolios.

Excessive trading on a variety of stocks can be confusing. If you want your investment dollars spread across companies and industries, and you either do not have enough money to spread around, or you have the money, but not the time, consider mutual funds. **Mutual funds** are investment companies whereby the investments are chosen and managed by the fund manager or team of managers. It is typical for a mutual fund to own tens of stocks and trade often.

While relieved that Gloria was not expecting an answer tomorrow, he began to doubt whether he could be prepared in one week.

In the meantime he would snoop around CCAM to get some answers. For his three stocks, he decided to place his orders another time, after he had more confidence in his ability to time the market. He put his file in his briefcase, but took Gloria's file to his bedroom. "There ain't nothin' wrong with a man who appreciates wealth in a woman!" he assured himself as he slipped the file under his pillow and turned off the lights.

ACB Year 3 Events

B-Innovation Magazine, September – "…ACB Holdings, Inc…has filed for a public offering of up to 100,000 shares of previously **restricted** Class A common stock. With a recent stock price…of $15.125, the proposed offering is slated to generate between $1.5 and $1.6 million in new cash…proceeds from the offering will be used to establish the Educational Foundation…The company's outstanding shares do not pay a dividend, but ACB boast a 13.05% return on assets and a 17.70% return on equity, with a debt to equity ratio of 16.98%." September 30 –High $16.125, Low $16.125 Close $16.125, Vol. 200

October 3 – ACB begins broadcasting to South African audiences. High $16.25, Low $16.25, Close $16.25, Vol 1300

October 4 – High, low, close at $16.25 Vol 200

Year 4

Give someone stock and they may have wealth for a day. Teach them how to invest and they may create wealth for generations.

Politics, War & Love

Julene Jamison was Julene Hombers before she married Marcus. She was proud of the Hombers name because she thought it was unique to her family (she had never met anyone else with that name). Before meeting Marcus, she was engaged to be married to her high school sweetheart. They had set the date for the year after she graduated from college, but in her senior year, she met Marcus, and there was suddenly no one else.

Julene was the kind of young woman many men would want to take to a public function. She was striking: tall, "big-boned" with a short Afro. She was on the track team, an honors student, politically active, and popular for being passionate about "her people." Her classmates thought she would go on to Harvard Law School or Howard University Medical School, but Julene had other interests.

The 1960s and 1970s were tough years on college campuses. Blacks were attending college in greater numbers than ever, and many students were concerned about the draft and the

U.S. involvement in Vietnam. Tension was everywhere, and political identity was determined by who your friends were. It was a time when you had to know if someone was your comrade or your foe. Were they part of the problem and supporting a military industrial complex bent on oppressing colored and poor people throughout the world or were they actively opposing the establishment? For the first time, Black Radicals and White Liberals converged on one major issue they could cooperate on opposition to: The Vietnam War.

Marcus Jamison, a conservative business student at the time, was finally led to speak at a rally:

I received a letter in the mail today, saying that I am supposed to report for military duty. I find it interesting that this so-called democracy thinks it has the moral authority to call me to military service, given that they've kept us from living to our full potential as men for centuries. Now, they think we have a duty to serve a country whose sole purpose is the exploitation of black and colored people throughout the world. Well, I say they don't have the right to call me to do anything I don't want to do. I would be happy to serve this nation in the high-rise ghettos they've built, the farms they've raped, the hospitals where we've gotten sub-standard care. Yes, wherever we have experienced subjugation, that is where you'll find me, serving my people...

The crowd roared, and this young man, articulate and handsome, wearing a closely cropped Afro and a necktie, captivated

Julene. He did not look like a radical, nor did he speak like one, but some purity of purpose must have driven him to stand atop a car talking about moral authority.

And one more thing. There comes a time when a boy becomes a man. We don't always know when that is going to be. Some people think that becoming a man is related to raging hormones, others think it has to do with the license to drive, or the ability to walk into a bar and have a drink. None of that matters in the making of a man. What matters is whether the man-child knows the challenges facing him, and chooses to take the path of greatest resistance – not to be part of the 'in' crowd – not because it makes the man-child feel good, but because he can handle the pain.

The crowd roared again.

But my brothers and sisters, what could be more painful than war? Are we men of conscience afraid of war? No, we are afraid of the men we might become as the result of an unjust war. For if you can kill without conscience, you are nothing more than a dog, and destined to live the rest of your life on all fours. That is what an unjust war will reduce you to!

The crowd was moved politically, and Julene was moved romantically. Later that day, she called her fiancé to discuss postponing their wedding.

Cycles, Ceilings & Charts

It had been four years since Marcus's death, and not a day had gone by that she did not think of him. But it was always on the way to B.B.'s office that she thought of him most. She wondered where he had hidden the $100,000 to invest in ACB and why he had never told her about it. It just did not make sense to her, though so many things seemed right when he was alive.

Meeting with B.B. was a struggle. While she did not always understand him during the meeting, she felt she was learning valuable lessons. After four years she was beginning to feel more comfortable talking about investments with him. This time she had some specific questions to ask him: why had he purchased additional stocks without telling her? She did not know whether to be mad at him or mad at herself for granting him full discretion to trade in her account. Maybe it was time to re-evaluate their relationship in light of the fact that she felt freer, emotionally, to begin taking control of her life, including her investments.

Julene entered the old elevator that seemed to get louder and louder every year. As she entered his office, as always, his assistant took a break. Julene wondered if the assistant ever learned anything since she was always out of the office during B.B.'s client meetings. Or was she just expected to leave when Julene was there?

B.B. always smiled when he saw Julene. He was glad to see this relatively young widow of Reverend Jamison make it on her own. He had seen so many women completely dependent on their husbands for financial support. He did not want her to suffer in his absence.

Rather than reach for her hand, B.B. gently hugged her, and Julene, though not offended, was taken aback. She had come to know B.B. as a cranky old man. Her agenda that day was to find out why he had purchased so many stocks.

B. B. explained to her that he had not purchased additional shares of stock – she had not given him any money, and he had not sold any shares to have cash to reinvest. She showed him the statement where the number of stocks she had in one company had doubled, the other tripled. B.B. was tempted to tell Julene a story about Tammy Freeman, but realized that Julene was excited and ready to listen without the weight of his family's history.

"Oh, now I see why there is so much excitement around splits. I had heard a lot of people talking about this or that company splitting, and I didn't really know what all that meant."

Julene wondered whether Marcus had known about splits, and why ACBN had not split. Before asking B.B., she looked at the price ACBN was purchased at, and asked B.B. for the current price. She concluded that ACBN did not need to split

A **stock split** is an increase in a corporation's number of outstanding shares of stock without any change in the shareholders' equity or the aggregate market value at the time of the split. In a split the share price declines. Directors of a corporation will authorize a split to make stock ownership more affordable to a broader base of investors.

For example, if a stock at $100 par value splits 2-for-1, the number of outstanding shares doubles (for example, from 10 million to 20 million) and the price per share drops by half, to $50. A holder of 50 shares before the split now has 100 shares at the lower price. If the same stock splits 4-for-1, the number of shares quadruples to 40 million and the share price falls to $25. Dividends per share also fall proportionately.

because the stock price seemed attractive, even more so than it was when Marcus bought it. Did Marcus invest in ACB because he thought it was an attractive investment or because he wanted to invest in a Black-owned company? She wanted to honor his objectives, but now it was her money *and* her decisions.

"So how's ACBN?" she asked B.B. "It closed yesterday at 22."

Stock price quotes, without additional information, only represent another movement in a trend of prices. To determine whether the stock price is "good" or a good value or cheap, look beyond the price and look at the price relative to the earnings – the **price earnings ratio**. The **P/E** is calculated by dividing the stock's closing price by a company's per share earnings over the last four quarters. The P/E *may* be listed in the stock pages. A P/E of 20 or lower has been considered a good value. However, a good value alone is not an indicator of stock price appreciation potential.

"I've got some good news for you!" He shows her a chart:

"Do you know what this means? Think back to the cotton plant."

Julene thought back to it, but did not understand the relevance.

"The stems are growing upward. I see a trend, and I expect that it will continue to increase for a while." B.B. continued, "Let's engage in a little technical analysis. In other words, let's try to identify a trend, so that we can make better decisions about when to buy and sell."

B.B. removed paper from his Jamison file, and showed it to Julene. "Reverend Jamison started here." He points to $23.50. "And you are here – around January, February. What do you see?"

ACBN March, 1994 - September, 1995

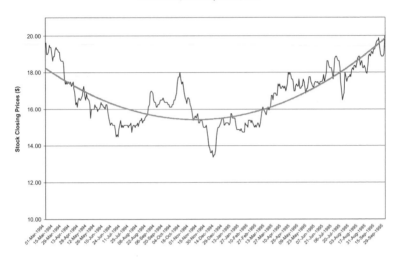

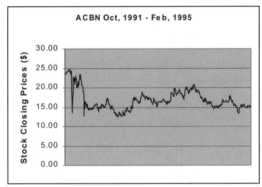

"I see that no money has been made in four years and that I probably should have sold when the price was at $20. Who knows if it'll ever get back to where it was?" Julene responded.

"Is that all you see? Do you remember those cotton plant drawings from our very first meeting?" B.B. began drawing furiously.

"Yes, but I tried to forget that meeting! Frankly B.B., we thought you were a little strange."

B.B. paused and peered over his coke-bottle glasses. "Had you all ever thought to ask me why I tell these stories? Julene, I mean no offense, but your sons? When I shook their hands at our first meeting, I knew that they didn't know the first thing about hard work. Their palms were soft and supple and the backs of their hands had been lotioned down so much – well you know what I'm getting at. They wanted me to tell them how to become wealthy as if they were entitled to it. Their hands told me that they didn't know a thing about hard work and sacrifice. So, I thought I'd impart a little history to help them understand that the best wealth-builders are those who know the meaning of hard, hard work. And you Julene, I know Marcus took care of you for 21 years while you raised your boys. That's not a luxury most people have these days. So when you come in here judging me and my surroundings, remember this — I won't help you to be better off in the future if you ignore the past."

Julene began to see B.B. in a completely different context. Once an eccentric old man, B.B. was now a purposeful sage.

"Now, please pay attention this time. I'm not going to repeat this again. Let me explain what I see. There are all kinds of charts, but I'm just going to show you two."

B.B. points to the chart, "This is a bar chart. The top of the vertical line is the highest price on that day. The bottom of the vertical is the lowest price that day. The tick to the left is the opening price, and the tick to the right is the closing price."

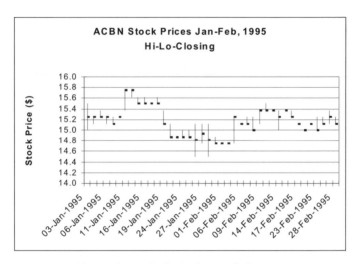

*Bar Chart: Shows the high, low and closing prices
of the stock each day.*

"This is a line chart. There are no opening or closing ticks, not even the highs and lows, just the closing prices. I like using this type of chart because it's generally easier to spot trends, and the closing price, at least theoretically, shows who's willing to hold

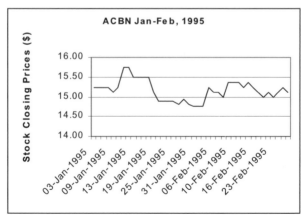

Line Chart: Shows the closing prices of the stock each day.

the stock overnight or over the weekend. These people supposedly have a strong belief that there is something more to ACBN

An historical market perspective gives you a better understanding of your stock's price and a context for understanding the relationships between current events and their effect on the whole market.

Business Cycles. Long-term business cycles conventionally consist of four stages: expansion, peak, contraction, and trough.

An **expansion** is characterized by an increase in business activity throughout the economy as a whole.
The **peak** occurs when the expansion is at the top of the cycle. The peak is often referred to as the stage of prosperity.
The **contraction**, the opposite of expansion, begins after the peak and is characterized by a decline in business activity.
The **trough** is the opposite of the peak, and is characterized by a stoppage of the decline.

than meets the eye. Basically, ACBN has been in a long-term downward trend. Once a long-term trend reverses, the turnaround has greater implications. There is no guarantee that there will be a reversal, but if there is one it will probably last for awhile."

B.B. took away the two charts, and briefly showed her another chart.

"Let's use this as an example of the broader market. Focus on years 1991 to 1994. What do you see? Over a three-year period, there was a **primary trend** upward in the market. A primary trend usually lasts between several months and a couple of years. If you are investing for the long term, as you are Julene, you want to know whether you are at the beginning or the end of the primary trend. If it is at the end, you will be invested when the down cycle begins and, depending on your goals, you may

Yetunde

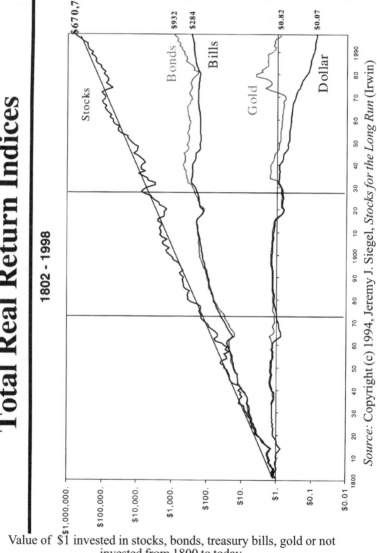

Total Real Return Indices

1802 - 1998

Value of $1 invested in stocks, bonds, treasury bills, gold or not invested from 1800 to today.

Source: Copyright (c) 1994, Jeremy J. Siegel, *Stocks for the Long Run* (Irwin) Reproduced with permission from The McGraw-Hill Companies.

not want to do that. The question is, without having seen the future, how do you know if you're at the beginning, in the middle or at the end of a trend? Basically, we are looking for ups *and* downs in business cycles."

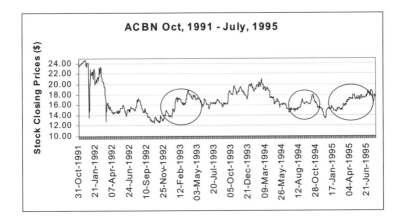

B.B. asked Julene if the prices in the circles meant anything to her. She examined what B.B. had highlighted, but she did not know what to say about those areas.

"Let's look at it in context. In March, 1992, your stock hit an all-time low of $12 per share. A low price alone doesn't signal a reversal of a downward trend. You would want to look at a few things like the overall market, stock prices in the same business segment, and of course, the length of the trend. What we're looking for is something like this." B.B. pointed to the chart below.

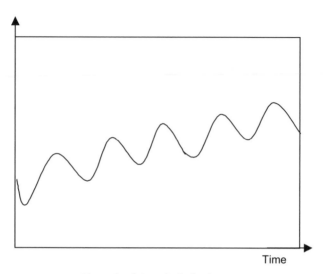

Every high is a little higher.

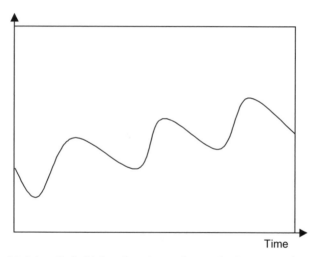

Every high is a little higher, but the peaks are farther apart than the peaks in the chart above.

"The more difficult challenge is determining the impact or significance of the reversal. Let's look at it in terms of love and infatuation." Julene sighed, as B.B. continued, "Infatuation is momentary. You may not know it at the time, but after it's over, you move on. Love usually takes time, but once it's there, it can last a lifetime. Infatuation makes you emotional. You become obsessed, and you may say and do things 'in the moment' that you wouldn't do normally. Love makes you stop and think before acting. Infatuation is a short-term trend. Love is a long-term or primary trend, and between infatuation and love is something like courting. You're certainly infatuated, but the feelings last longer than a crush. That's an intermediate trend."

B.B. continued, "Short-term trends usually last a few weeks, intermediate-term trends can last several weeks to several months, and primary trends can last several months to a few years. The most significant trend lasts for several years (that's a marriage), and that is called a secular trend. As I said, the trend is not always easy to determine because there is no set rule that says a primary trend can only last so many months or years, but this will give you a general framework to begin your own analysis."

Julene was beginning to understand. "How do you know when a trend is changing?" she asked.

B.B. was delighted to see her interest. "I thought you'd never ask! Basically, we need to look at support and resistance lines. It is at these lines that one could possibly predict a temporary change in the trend. I'll start by drawing two lines on this next chart.

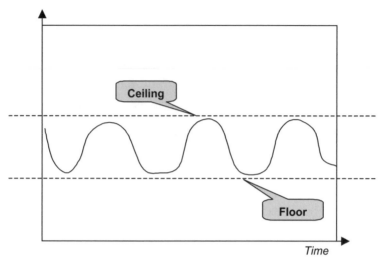

"The resistance is the ceiling and the support is the floor. These usually indicate a trading range. When a stock breaks through the ceiling or the floor, a reversal is likely to come soon after. Do you understand anything about volume?" he asked.

Julene nodded affirmatively, thinking back on when she first began reading the stock pages, but she was not completely confident in her answer.

"Volume is about the number of shares traded. When you look at the volume, you're trying to determine the enthusiasm of the investors who are trading (buyers and sellers). If volume is up, and the price of the stock is up too, the chances for spotting a reversal in the trend are better. And when the volume and price go

LESSON FOURTEEN: Focus not only on price trends, but volume trends too.

You may be able to identify a change in the perception of the stock before the price changes.

in opposite directions, you get a so-called 'advanced notice' that a potential trend reversal is in the works." B.B. asked in his most assuring voice, "And you know prices can go up or down dramatically and swiftly, right?"

Julene again nodded affirmatively.

"Okay, the more stock being exchanged at particular volumes, and the faster the change in price from the former price movement, the more significant the support and resistance levels are. The more you look at charts, the more you'll be able to spot patterns, and make determinations about timing. Just recall the story I told you about the cotton plant, and you'll be okay."

No one really times the market well *all* the time. In other words, rarely do investors buy stock at the lowest possible price, and sell at the highest possible price. Sometimes panic strikes and investors sell prematurely. Conventional wisdom suggests that if you stay in the market a long time (at least five years) with quality stocks, the stock prices may weather the storm and appreciate at a reasonable rate over time.

"Let's take a look at another situation: ACBN's highs and volumes since its first year. It's a little difficult to draw the resistance line and the support line because there's no easily identifiable pattern. Notice how high the volume was when your husband bought the stock in the first year. Notice the prices. The price fell from $23.50 in February to $15 about two months later, but the volume pretty much stayed the same. What that tells you is that there wasn't a lot of enthusiasm or excitement around trading – that even though the price fell, that wasn't reason enough for most shareholders to begin selling a lot of their shares." B.B. looked up from his papers to make sure Julene was with him.

"Now let's jump over to January through May. The price
went from $18 to $20 in two months, then back down to about
$18. The prices were going up while the volume was going down.
When this happens it is usually because buyers are trading when
there is a lack of pressure to sell. Eventually, this type of buying
will cause the stock price to increase to a level that will inspire a
sell-off – when shareholders sell some shares to make a profit.
After the sell-off, prices tend to drop dramatically – notice that
the price dropped down in June and July, generating an increase
in volume. The biggest problem here is that it's difficult to spot
trends when too few people are selling the stocks they own, and
only a few are buying the stock. There just isn't enough enthusiasm one-way or the other. Ideally, we should be looking for
heads and shoulders.

"This is the head, and these are the shoulders. When the
head is down, the trend is that prices are expected to rise. It is no
guarantee, because anything can happen. The Federal Reserve
Board, the Feds, might raise interest rates, Donald Jackson might
resign, ACB may make a poor business move, anything can happen. But if you want to get an idea of whether your stock is going

Heads and shoulders patterns resemble the head and shoulders outline of a person. The pattern is supposed to signal a reversal of a trend. As prices move down to the right shoulder, a head and shoulders top is formed, meaning that prices should be falling. A reverse head and shoulders pattern has the head at the bottom of the chart, meaning the prices should be rising.

north, at least for the short term, look for the head and shoulders, and that should tell you whether the trend is up or down."

Julene looked at the chart. She had never really looked at a chart before, at least not in a way that she could tell anything from it. Pointing to December, 1994 through May, 1995, she asked if B. B. knew why ACBN was on its way up.

He could not tell her why, except that earlier in the year, ACBN's high and low were very close, around $14 and $15 a share when it had been around $18 in late fall.

"Remember when we met last year, and I said that ACBN had gone from about $16 to about $18 in two months. It was

Sometimes, there is no easily discernable reason why a few investors take an interest in a stock, except that perhaps more people have become aware of the opportunity to buy the stock and they want to own it before others begin buying it.

because ACBN was at a low for the year. And then maybe it was because of the 100,000 shares offered on behalf of the foundation. Maybe a little goodwill was good for the stock price. Maybe not. Maybe it was the result of the market going up in general. Sometimes investors just buy a stock they think is at a low price, *if* they do not think it will go any lower."

Julene had no idea what he meant by the "general market," but she did not want him to think that after four years of investing, she didn't really understand the "general market." B.B. knew she didn't know, just by looking at her face. He didn't want her to feel insecure, so he proceeded as if he was having a conversation with a more confident and sophisticated investor.

"Julene, some investors really don't care what's going on in the domestic economy, let alone the world. All they care about is whether they are making money. But for some people, they want to evaluate the success or failure of their portfolio relative to the market. The way they do that is by looking at an index.

"Now the Dow is the granddaddy of the indexes. It's been around since the late 1800s, and is kept by *The Wall Street Journal*. If you listen to or watch the news, they may quote an increase or decrease in the Dow, the S&P 500, or some other index that represents some other universe of stocks. I suggest you listen to whatever you hear, and that will keep you somewhat abreast of

---

An **index** measures the ups and downs of the stock market. Indexes are created and maintained by publishers of financial information, such as

- Dow Jones (Dow Jones Industrial Average Index or DJIA),
- S&P 500 (Standard and Poors)
- NASDAQ Composite (National Association of Securities Dealers Automated Quotation).
- Russell 2000
- Wilshire 5000

Indexes are often expressed in point or percentage changes, such as: "The DJIA was up...NASDAQ down and the S&P 500, up..."

Investors tend to measure the performance of their portfolio relative to the index or indexes of their choice. The "keepers" of the index are not obligated to keep the same composition of stocks, therefore, on occasion, it makes sense to know whether the composition has changed since you began following it.

daily developments."

"So, what if I hear that the Dow is up 50 points or down 150 points?" Julene wondered aloud what she had wondered silently for many years.

"Basically, any up or down movement means another movement, maybe inside or outside a trend. The Dow includes 30 companies. If the price of any one of the stocks goes up or down one point (or about one dollar), the index moves up or down about five points. This will change whenever the keepers of the index decide to change the computation. It is rare that they do, but when they do, they'll announce it and there will probably be some news coverage on it.

Julene was finally beginning to understand the big picture. "How long has this trend been going on?" B.B. reached for the historical chart again (See page 106).

LESSON FIFTEEN: Do not let an index alone dictate your investment objectives.

The NASDAQ Composite Index was especially noteworthy and newsworthy in 1999 because it closed the year up 85.6%. No other index in the history of indexing stocks had such an increase in one year. The dramatic increase was difficult to ignore. But in the year 2000 it began slipping downward.

"A very long time," he replied, pointing at the chart. "Julene, I've been meaning to ask you about your sons. How are they?"

Julene confirmed that they were employed, healthy and learning how to invest.

"May I ask how they are investing their money?"

Julene respectfully declined to answer specifically, "Each year, we review our portfolios to see who is becoming the better investor. I told them that I would give them each additional money if they proved they were good with their own money. To date, I haven't given them anything more."

B.B., as much as he respected and cared for Julene, wondered how she felt qualified to judge whether her sons were good investors, but did not dare ask.

"As a matter of fact, I'm going to see them this evening, and maybe this year they'll finally get it right."

Home to Roost

Later that evening, Julene and her sons gathered around the dining room table, as they had when they first saw Reverend Jamison's investment statements.

"The way I see it, this has been a good year economically, more Black folks are making money, we still watch a lot of TV and ACB has no competitors. I'm holding on," Ishmael stated.

"Fool, are you in this to lose money or make money?" countered Isaac.

"Make money, of course. So what if I sell it? What do I do next? Buy some other company's stock?"

"Yes, and I have the right ones," Isaac motions Ishmael to join him at the table to look at the stock pages.

"See how these stocks have gone up? This one, that one and this one?" Isaac points to different lines on the page. "Seems like there are hundreds that are better than ACBN. All I want is

52 Weeks					Yld		Vol				Net
					\%\						
Hi	Lo	Stock	Sym	Div	%	PE	100s	Hi	Lo	Close	Chg
					-A-A-A-						
32	23$^3/_{16}$	Ashanti	ACBN	--	--	--	1800	16	15 $^1/_4$	16	--
57	25$^3/_{16}$	Atella	ATL	--	--	6	80232	37 $^3/_4$	35 $^1/_8$	36 $^7/_{16}$	-$^3/_{16}$
68	43$^7/_8$	Azure	AZR	.64	1.1	--	2324	60 $^5/_8$	59 $^1/_4$	59 $^3/_8$	+$^9/_{16}$

NEW YORK STOCK EXCHANGE COMPOSITE TRANSACTIONS

Quotations as of 4 p.m. Eastern Time
March 12, 199-

for us to make some money."

"Me too, but what makes you think these companies will always be up and never down? I think that if I read the paper regularly, I'll know when to get out. How else would you know?" Ishmael was stumped.

"Well, if you don't trust me, trust yourself and trade online like I do. Or I guess you could call B.B. Freeman or some other broker and let him tell you when to sell it. Frankly, I don't trust Freeman – he's old, off-the-wall, and Black." Isaac caught himself. Julene and Ishmael were taken aback by Isaac's racist comment.

"What I mean is," Isaac rushed to say, "you don't see many Blacks in this business for some reason. He's not at a prestigious firm; his office is ugly and cramped. It just doesn't look good."

Ishmael just shook his head in disappointment.

"What are you shaking your head about?! If you'd give as much time to your investments as you do judging me, you'd be a lot better off," Isaac protested.

"Brother, I have given some thought to what I want to do, and I've decided I'm going to keep my account with B.B. until it doesn't make sense to. As a matter of fact, I begged him to meet with me because I figured that despite his stupid storytelling and his homely office, if Dad trusted him, he must be okay."

"Did he make Dad any money?" Isaac asked skeptically.

"Well, if you don't know the answer to that question, I don't know if you should be making your own investment decisions. Do you? I don't want you to lose money, if you're serious about having it. But Mr. Freeman's been around a long time. So, if he's willing to work with me and I only have a few shares, why not? If he says something that doesn't make sense, I won't do it."

Isaac, listening for once, felt foolish, and suggested that his brother continue working with Freeman.

Ishmael, always the "nice guy," decided to take advantage of his lead in the conversation, "Mom said that you're using a lot of fancy trading techniques on your stocks. You'd think you'd have more money than you do, given all the time you put into managing your portfolio."

"Ish – Man, I'm getting really tired of that trash talk. You've done nothing with your stocks – nada, zip, zilch – and yet you'll sit there and judge me because I haven't made a whole lot of money. But, brother, I've made some, which is more than I can say for your sorry investment philosophy of 'inherit and hold' no matter what! Man, no expert investor would ever advise you to do what you've done. Why don't you do something!? Anything!"

"Like what, sell?" Ishmael shouted. "Do you think I should place a sell stop limit once the price hits $23.50 and just call it even after four years of being in a bull market? Do you?" Ishmael was hot.

Isaac was shocked into silence that Ishmael knew anything about a sell stop limit, since he had never placed an order.

"Yeah, what are you looking at? You think you're the only one who knows how to trade, don't you?" Ishmael asked smugly.

"Ishmael, I have just one question. Where the heck have you been the last four years? In this bull market you could have invested in almost anything else and made lots of money. I bet even Freeman helped Mom make some money in some real conservative stuff, though she won't tell us what she's doing."

A **bull market** is a prolonged rise in the prices of stocks and is characterized by high trading volume. A bear market is just the opposite.

With great interest Julene watched her sons' competitive exchange. Would this be the year that Ishmael showed some interest in investing? Would Isaac learn restraint in his pursuits to become rich? She asked them to show her their recent statements.

"Isaac, I see real effort on your part to become a good trader. Ishmael, I see your effort to look deeper, to look beyond the numbers and seek out potential. I know you don't want to sell for the wrong reasons. I see a lot of effort, I really do, but again…"

"No cash. Right, Mom?" Isaac blurted out.

Ishmael, completely exasperated, asked his mother what she expected from them.

Julene replied, "Something a little more and something a little less than what I've seen."

Isaac wondered if she had been spending too much time with B.B. Freeman.

ACB Year 4 Events

 April 3 – High $17.375, Low $17.25 Close $17.25 Vol 1100

April 4 – ACB urges the FCC to scrap racial preferences in the auction of wireless communications licenses. High $17.375, Low $17.3125 Vol 7900

April 5 – High $17.250, Low $17.125 Close $17.125 Vol 400

November 1 – High $21.125, Low $20.75 Close$20.875 Vol 104800

November 2 – High $22.25, Low $21.125 Close $22.25 Vol 29500

The D.C. Courier, November 3 – ACB made offer to buy back $58 million (or 3 million shares representing 15% of the outstanding shares) of its stock from an Arrow-Mitchell unit (an early investor in the company) at $19.11 a share, the average price over the past 60 days.

November 3 – High $22.25, Low 22.00 close 22.25 Vol 8000

The Street Reports, December 14 – ACB completed the repurchase of 3,036,600 of its common shares held beneficially by New York-based Arrow-Mitchell, Inc. Following the repurchase, which ACB said it funded through cash reserves and credit facilities, the company has 16,679,805 shares outstanding.

December 13 – High $23.50, Low $23, Close $23 Vol 3400

December 14 – High $23.125, Low $23, Close $23.125 Vol 4100

The repurchase of millions of shares can be costly to a company. Determine whether the use of cash for this purpose significantly diminishes the company's ability to reinvest cash and grow the business

Year 5

Insularity can cause economic short-sightedness.

Ishmael's Getting Frustrated

Feeling extremely tired, Ishmael rose early to go to work. He wondered whether he was suffering from exhaustion. What was meant to be a good entry-level social worker's position had turned into a fundraising mission, a cause seemingly unrelated to helping the drug-addicted get back on their feet.

As he approached the shower, he began to think of what he would wear that day. When he first started at DRC (Drug Recovery Center), he could wear whatever he wanted, but now, things had changed. A cheap tie, an old jacket and black jeans. But what shirt? In 1991, he had no idea that five years later he would be executive director of DRC. "I can't believe I'm doing this!" he would often say as he fixed his tie. He even cut his locks to be more presentable to funders.

As much as Ishmael could not believe he went from being a good counselor to a mediocre administrator, others knew that he was the best person for the job. He was organized, had a vision of a healthier inner Houston, was passionate and persuasive when he wanted assistance, and could rally the troops to tough it out when they did not know if they would get paid that week.

He did not apply for the job; the board begged him to take it. The treasurer approached him, "Ishmael, you know we've had funding problems every year, but whenever you get involved in the process, the money just seems to come in. Why is that?" Maybe it was because of his father's lasting influence that people wanted to give money to a good cause, or maybe he really was more talented than he had originally thought.

After his shower, he chose the white shirt to go with his new "monkey suit" and hopped on his bike.

"Darn!" he swore to himself. Hot, humid weather and a bike ride insured a wet uniform by the time he got to the office. Ishmael wondered when he would be able to buy a decent car; when he would have the means to take a woman out for a great time; and when he could stop thinking about how little he had.

Wiping his brow as he entered the DRC lobby, Ishmael found what seemed like hundreds of clients in need of help. They all rose to their feet and scurried after him as if they had just witnessed the Second Coming. Ishmael knew they held him in high esteem, because he could save them from the hell of drug addiction and deliver them to a sober life everlasting. He had had a few successes, but not enough to think he was any more of a man than they were. He was just lucky to have good parents who scared him away from drugs.

"Patience, fellas. Folks will be with y'all soon. Just take your seats, okay?" Ishmael was frustrated, and during these moments, he told himself that they would never listen to him. How could they? They only wanted drugs or to get off drugs. All that talk about patience and waiting your turn meant nothing to someone whose sole survival depended on an artificial substance.

In the social work field Ishmael had achieved a career level that usually required advanced degrees: management. Yet, he found it ironic that as he climbed the ladder of not-for-profit success, the community he served fell down the ladder, again and again. He saw improvements in most of those he worked with, but the number of addicts kept growing, and the number of clients diagnosed with HIV or full-blown AIDS was increasing. It was depressing, and it was getting to him.

What depressed him most was that his clients were almost all totally financially dependent on others to help them through recovery. Barely getting by themselves, they had to turn to charity, governmental, and not-for-profit handouts to make it through. What if all these generous entities said, "Enough! To hell with them all!" What would they do then, he wondered.

His own financial situation was not much better. After five years in his profession, he still had not saved any money. Without touching his ACBN stock, he lived pay-check to pay-check. Maybe that was why he was so good at making sure the funding was in on time – he could not miss getting paid. He knew the day might come when the funding dried up and contemplated his next career move. One thing was sure: it did not involve financial insecurity.

Should he sell his ACBN stock before it went down again? After five years, it was time to seek B.B. Freeman's professional advice. Pushing his fund-raising proposals aside, he reached for the phone. He left a message, loosened his necktie noose then turned to the papers on his desk, and proceeded to "push" them – longing for a well-paying job to counsel those in distress.

The Light Finally Comes On

Thank God for Saturdays, Ishmael thought. At least he could think about himself for once. And today, he would think about learning something else about investing. A few months previous, Ishmael made a resolution that was long in the making: he would commit the next year to learning as much as he could about investing, then make an educated decision to sell ACBN or buy more (not an option he had considered before).

He began looking for the stock sections in *Mahogany* and *Flight* because those magazines were readily available in his office. He found nothing there. Then he realized that his father died reading *The Houston Chronicle*, and presumably that was how he first heard of ACB. However, there was no stock information in the business section.

Frustrated that he could not find any Black publications with stock pages, Ishmael called Jerri, his friend at the State University library, and asked her to tell him which major black publications regularly reported on the stock market. Jerri mentioned all the well-known names. None of the publications regularly reported on the stock market, if they ever did.

Somehow, Ishmael could understand their situation. The purpose of those papers was to address issues around being Black in America, and, as far as he knew, they did a good job. But what about business news? Would reporting on corporate business affairs fall outside the interest of Black folks and if so, why? Given that answers were not forthcoming, he focused on where he was going to find information about investing.

In one of the many books he borrowed from the library, Ishmael stumbled upon a chart that showed the growth of $1 from 1800 to 1996…

He examined it carefully, and was ashamed that he did not know more about the long-term trend he just saw. But don't be hard on yourself, he thought, given his lack of interest in money issues. He looked at the chart again.

1913 – Federal Reserve System established
1932 – Bottom of the stock market crash during
          The Great Depression
1939 – Beginning of World War II
1940 – War between the U.S. and Japan began
1941 – First nuclear chain reaction
1961 – Bay of Pigs
1962 – Cuban Missile Crisis
1965 – Six-Day War in the Middle East

If one dollar could become $0.07 or $670,760 over a nearly 200-year period, then that was great, he thought. However, the stock market might not be the best way to evaluate the economic successes of Black people coming from slavery, to sharecropping, to owning businesses in the South, to migrating during the industrial age, to becoming college-educated, to owning businesses and working in "the professions." He began to see the chart in a different way:

1865 – 13th Amendment to the U.S. Constitution, Section 1. "Neither slavery nor involuntary servitude, except as a punishment for crime whereof the party shall have been duly convicted, shall exist within the United States, or any place subject to their jurisdiction."

1868 – 14th Amendment of the U.S. Constitution, Section 1. "…No State shall make or enforce any law which shall abridge the privileges or immunities of citizens of the United States, nor shall any State deprive any person of life, liberty, or property, without due process of law; nor deny to any person within its jurisdiction the equal protection of the laws."

1900 – Black Capitalism became a social movement, endorsed by W.E.B. DuBois and Booker T. Washington's National Negro Business League.

1925 – A. Philip Randolph organized the Brotherhood of Sleeping Car Porters.

1929 – National Negro Business League was founded.

1932 – Cotton sold for 6 cents a pound and a sharecropper made $270 per 45 acres of cotton picked. Southern Blacks began migrating to the North.

1939 – NAACP Legal Defense and Educational Fund was organized.

1944 – United Negro College Fund was founded.

1954 – *Brown* vs. *Board of Education of Topeka, Kansas* – U.S. Supreme Court ruled that racial segregation in public schools is unconstitutional. Desegregation in U.S. Armed Forces is completed.

1960 – Student Non-Violent Coordinating Committee (SNCC) is organized. President Eisenhower signed the Voting Rights Act of 1960.

1961 – The term "affirmative action" first entered public discourse in the Executive Order that created the Equal Employment Opportunity Commission (EEOC).

1963 – Whitney Young, Jr., president of The Urban League, called for "more than equal rights" for blacks. March on Washington.

1964 – Congress passed the Economic Opportunity Act that created Head Start, Upward Bound and college work-study financial aid programs.

1969 – The National Black Economic Development Conference adopted the Black Manifesto.

1970 – The Race Relations Information Center in Nashville, TN reported three Black executives among 3,182 senior officers of the top 50 corporations in the U.S. (Robert C. Weaver of Metropolitan Life Insurance Company; Clifton R. Wharton, Jr. of Equitable Life Assurance; and Thomas A. Wood of Chase Manhattan). Parks Sausage Company (a Black-owned company) trades on the National Association of Securities Dealers Automated Quotation exchange (NASDAQ).

1991 – ACB Holdings, Inc. goes public on NYSE.

The relevance of the market in the context of history fascinated Ishmael. Buoyed by affirmative action laws, the struggles of the 1960's revolved around Black equality and power. It seemed a logical progression that equal access to education led to equal access in business and career opportunities. While this debate was happening, the stock market started another upward trend, i.e. while people were embroiled in heated legal battles, the economy kept moving upward. Ishmael surmised that stock investors in the 1960's either believed that economic integration would ultimately be good for business, or that affirmative action and similar policies would not cause such social and economic havoc as to make businesses less profitable. He concluded it was both. At the same time that some parents were removing their children from integrated schools, many investors did not sell their stocks when Black employees were hired. Now, steeped with a stronger sense of the struggle for economic justice, Ishmael was committed to learning how to invest.

According to a 1997 study conducted by Edward N. Wolff, New York University, the richest 1% of Americans owned 51.4% of the outstanding stock, the next richest 9% owned 37%, and the other 90% of the population owned 11.6% of the outstanding stock.
(The Wall Street Journal, September 13, 1999)

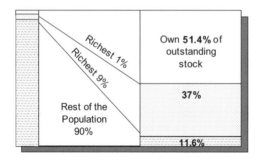

Ishmael put himself on a reading regimen. He read *The Street Reports* (when he could find one in the café) and *B-Innovation* Magazine regularly. Though the dailies did not provide much information about ACBN beyond the daily stock prices, he read the dailies to get a sense of the market as a whole. Due to the timing, he read the magazines for commentary and analysis, not news. The governmental reports lacked news, but included other details not available in the newspapers or magazines.

To really understand a company, Ishmael knew he would have to venture deeper than the magazines and newspapers. He began delving into the annual reports, 10Ks, and analyst reports written and published by companies. The main library had electronic copies and access to online versions of the 10K, but he had to call ACB for another copy of the annual report (As a shareholder he received the annual report every year, but had thrown them out.). Ishmael decided to study ACB's annual report and 10K from 1995.

A **10K** is an annual report required by the Securities and Exchange Commission (SEC) of every issuer of a registered security, every exchange-listed company, and any company with 500 or more shareholders or $1 million or more of gross assets. The form provides for disclosure of total sales, revenue, and pre-tax operating income, as well as sales by separate classes of products for each of a company's separate lines of business for each of the past five years.

Ishmael did not understand everything he read, nor did he understand all the implications of ACB's expansion into other areas by forming joint ventures with other companies. However, he was proud of himself for reading it, and knew that when his mother reviewed his portfolio this year, he could justify why he held the ACBN stock.

ACB HOLDINGS INC. 10-K

Item 1.   BUSINESS

GENERAL DEVELOPMENT OF BUSINESS

In connection with the initial public offering of its Class A common
stock, ACB Holdings, Inc. ("ACB Holdings") was incorporated in
Delaware in July 1991. As a result of a series of related transactions completed in September 1991, Ashanti Cable Broadcasting
Network, Inc. ("ACB"), a State of Washington corporation formed
in 1979, became a wholly owned subsidiary of ACB Holdings. In
November 1991, ACB Holdings completed its initial public stock
offering and...

After all the reading and studying, he realized his biggest ob-
stacle to building wealth: himself. In his present career, there was
little he could do to generate enough income to effect economic
change in the community. He imagined having an agency that had
enough money to give every client the best medical care and employment training. As it stood, the best he could do for today's
needs was ask for more money from people who either earned
lots of money, or invested larger sums.

Tired from his daylong mini-education, Ishmael closed the
last report. He patted himself on the back for applying his common sense to information he had never been exposed to before,
and promised himself that he would become more "numerically
inclined" in his next study session. After all, he had given himself
a year to figure it out.

Ishmael had started the morning exhausted by the weight of his personal economic pressures and feelings of guilt for thinking of leaving the DRC for a more lucrative job. His thoughts of successfully investing while serving the needy provided the relief he needed. Growing old and poor was not an option anymore. Investing would be the happy medium that would allow him to be with his people and take care of his long-term needs without reservation. For the first time in years, Ishmael began to feel good about his work, his ACBN stock and himself.

ACB Year 5 Events

The Street Reports, March – April Martin was appointed to the new post of president and chief operating officer. She was the executive vice president of strategic business development, general counsel and corporate secretary. High $30.625, Low $30.375 Close $30.50 Vol 20800
March 20 – High $31.50, Low $30.50, Close $30.75 Vol 11700
Analysts found that ACBN's cable division made profits; everything else resulted in losses.

B-Innovation Magazine, April – Ashanti Cable Broadcasting Network will be opening its first theme-based coffee shop chain in Seattle in October. Called ACB Café, the new restaurant will be located in the Queen Anne district.

B-Innovation Magazine, May – …Ashanti Cable Broadcasting Network and SoftMicro have formed a joint venture in cyberspace: a new Web site offering called ACB-SM…The idea for the alliance grew from a desire to close the "digital divide" by providing the 5.5 million African-Americans who have cable television with a reason to go online…

The Street Reports, August 7 – Maxwell Sharpes, ACBN VP and "insider" sold 556,000 shares at 22.1, which equaled 100% of his holdings in ACB.

August 6 – High $24.375, Low $24, Close $24.375 Vol 4300

August 7 – High $24.25, Low $23.50 Close $24 Vol 16500

August 8 – High 24, Low $23.875 Close $24 Vol 26000

Insider trading may affect the price of shares depending on who is selling, how much, the theory behind the sell-off and whether the selling is consistent with a particular pattern of selling.

September 25 - ACBN and ApplauseApplauseMedia Corporation announce that they will launch the nation's first movie channel that showcases African-American movie artists, called ACBN Movies/GALAXY.

September 25 – Donald Jackson sold 820,000 shares representing 29% of his holdings in ACB for a price of $23.75 each. High $29.75, Low $27.875, Close $29.75 Vol 15700

September 26 – High $29.75, Low $29.00, Close $29.00 Vol 11700

October 10 – High $28.75, Low $28.625, Close $28.625 Vol 1000
October 11 – ACB reported that fiscal fourth-quarter earnings climbed 8.1% due to an increase in advertising and subscriber revenue. For the 4th quarter ended July 31, earnings rose to $5.3 million, or 30 cents a share, from $4.9 million or 25 cents a share, a year earlier. Revenue rose 16% to $34.8 million from $30 million, a year earlier. High $28.875, Low $28.75, Close $28.875 Vol 700
October 14 – High $29.25, Low $28.875, Close $29.125 Vol 7800

The Street Reports, November 16 – ACBN and Roasted Bean Resorts announced that they formed a joint venture to explore the feasibility of buying land to build a chain of theme-based coffee shops, aimed at the more than 2.2 million African-Americans who visit Seattle every year. ACBN is available in 46.4 million households.
November 18 – High $27.875, Low $27.625 Close $27.875 Vol 1600

D.C. Courier, December 14 – Labor Relations Board adjudged that ACB acted illegally when it threatened to eliminate the workers' jobs.
December 16 – High $26.75, Low $26.625 Close $26.625 Vol 800

Year 6

The ultimate revolution is to come full circle.

My, How Things Change

B.B. was in his office thumbing through some of his memorabilia when he came across the *Black Manifesto*, a document he helped draft in 1969.

Black Manifesto

We the black people assembled in Detroit, Michigan, for the National Black Economic Development Conference are fully aware that we have been forced to come together because racist white America has exploited our resources, our minds, our bodies, our labor. For centuries we have been forced to live as colonized people inside the United States, victimized by the most vicious, racist system in the world. *We have helped to build the most industrialized country in the world.*

We are therefore demanding of the white Christian churches and Jewish synagogues, which are part and parcel of the system of capitalism, that they begin to pay reparations to black people in this country…This demand for $500,000,000 is not an idle resolution or empty words. Fifteen dollars for every nigger in the United States is only a beginning of the reparations due us as people who have been exploited and degraded, brutalized, killed and persecuted. Underneath all of this exploitation, the racism of this country has produced a psychological effect upon us that we are beginning to shake off. We are no longer afraid to demand our full rights as a people in this decadent society.

We are demanding $500,000,000 to be spent in the following way:

- We call for the establishment of a southern land bank to help our brothers and sisters who have to leave their land because of racist pressure, and for people who want to establish cooperative farms but who have no funds...
- We call for the establishment of four major publishing and printing industries...
- We call for the establishment of four of the most advanced scientific and futuristic audio-visual networks...
- We call for a research skills center, which will provide research on the problems of black people...
- We call for the establishment of a training center for the teaching of skills in community organization, photography, movie making, television making and repair, radio building and repair and all other skills needed in communication...
- We recognize the role of the National Welfare Rights Organization, and we intend to work with them...
- We call for $20,000,000 to establish a National Black Labor Strike and Defense Fund...
- We call for the establishment of the International Black Appeal (IBA)...The IBA is charged with producing more capital for the establishment of cooperative businesses in the United States and in Africa, our Motherland...

We call for the establishment of a black university...

In order to win our demands, we are aware that we will need massive support, therefore:

We call upon all black people throughout the United States to consider themselves as members of the National Black Economic Development Conference...

Source: Excerpts from The National Black Economic Development Conference, 1969 quoted in Schuchter, Arnold, Reparations: The Black Manifesto and Its Challenge to White America, *1970*

B.B. was astonished. It had been thirty years since he met with the progressive and revolutionary activists of his day. But at the moment, he could not feel the anger expressed in the document. He marveled at the thought that his approach to achieving economic fairness was to make "White Christians and Jews" pay Blacks $500,000,000 for slavery, discrimination and intolerance. He thought about Tobi, Thomas, his parents and all their struggles combined. He began to remember the anger he felt 30 years ago. Then suddenly, the anger disappeared.

He looked around his office to judge himself – post Black Manifesto. There were photographs of his younger self, though middle-aged at the time, sporting a salt and pepper Afro. One picture showed him standing in front of the building that housed his Appian Street office. Another picture included his fraternity brothers taken at their reunion at Hampton. One with his wife. And another one, taken at a rally, gloved fist clinched and raised high above his head. Throughout the years the photographs had all yellowed from the direct sun and his own lack of attention.

He turned back to the Manifesto and thought that, ironically, he had become an agent of the same capitalist system he protested then. What changed – are you part of the problem, or part of the solution? Did you sell out, Comrade Freeman? "No," his words gave little consolation, "the problems were – are real, I just found a different solution."

He rose from his desk and walked over to the copier and made a copy for Ishmael with a note attached.

Ishmael,

I think I understand where you're coming from and why you haven't met with me alone. Why don't you bring your brother to the office and I'll treat you both to lunch. I want to talk with you both about your goals in life.

Yours in the struggle,

B.B. Freeman

As he placed the manifesto and his note in an envelope, B.B. regretted that he and his wife had chosen not to have children – young Freemans to inherit his business and the family legacy.

Strength in Numbers

Isaac was excited about driving to Houston to see Ishmael. It had been almost two years since he met Gloria and he wondered what she would be doing while he was visiting his twin. They had been virtually inseparable since their second meeting when he thought he was dazzling her with his knowledge of investing in the stock market, and she thought he was at least considerate enough to try to impress her. He felt secure that they were on the right track, but knew that he had not achieved the career success she had, and therefore did not feel quite worthy of a commitment from her.

Isaac was more concerned about Ishmael. He loved Ishmael and was grateful for having Ishmael as that sobering and whole-some influence in his life. No one knew him like Ishmael. He never felt he had to explain who he was deep down, because deep down, they shared the same fundamental thoughts, had the same vision for a better world, and had the same taste in women ("if she's not like Julene, she's not marriage material"). Ishmael was the most generous, down-for-the-people-for-real kind of brother (he must have gotten that from Dad). Isaac found com-fort in the fact that Ishmael felt the same way about him, even though they were competitive at times.

Ishmael and Isaac agreed that their "Twins Weekend" would be the best. The rules were only the two of them, hanging out, having fun, supporting each other, no competition, lots of good eating and drinking and talking investments. Isaac knew that Ishmael would not be able to resist gloating about the success of ACBN, but that was okay because Isaac was all ears for a good investment opportunity.

As he approached Tubman Village he frowned. He did not understand why Ishmael would not move to a nicer neighbor-hood. "Do you have to live with the addicts in order to help them?" he wondered aloud. Tubman Village wasn't anything like this growing up, but he understood why Ishmael returned to the place where he used to live – he saw a generation of folks moving back-wards rather than ahead, and thought he could be a positive ex-ample just by being there every day. Isaac reached for the CD changer controls, "Maybe it wasn't such a bright idea to drive this brand new car around here.

He slowed down and watched his surroundings more carefully. The liquor store was still there, but the grocery market and laundromat were closed. No businesses had been established in their places. Isaac had wanted to buy a cold six-pack to start off "Twins Weekend," but he had to drive several blocks past Ishmael's place to find a store where he felt safe. He drove over two miles until he found a strip mall. He was proud to see Black folks rebuilding the community. He parked, set the alarm, and walked into the grocery store. As he approached the cash register with his six-pack, he realized, sadly, that the stores were probably not Black-owned – there was not one Black cashier or clerk. On his way back to Ishmael's, he decided that Ishmael could and should live in better surroundings, and that he would support him in that endeavor...if that was what Ishmael really wanted to do.

Cooperation Not Competition

Like a pre-dawn duel at the OK Corral, the twins whipped out their portfolios. Isaac's was in a three-ringed, leather-bound binder filled with colored and numbered tabs. Ishmael's was a pocket folder with only one sheet of paper – his most recent quarterly statement. They shook hands to seal their promise that they would not compete with each other. They would try to learn from each other's successes and failures. Ishmael, though, could not wait to begin.

"Twin, have you been following ACBN this year? It's trading at about 35! I knew it would happen eventually, I just didn't think it would take as long as it did. Brother Jackson is making a whole lot of Black folks happy. So what do you think?" Ishmael finished in a rush.

"To be honest with you, I don't know what to think. I don't really know ACB because I've always thought that folks wouldn't invest in it Tell me what you know." Isaac, sincerely interested, was curious what his twin, who had not made a trade in six years, would have to say.

Ishmael pulled out a booklet and said, "Let's start with ACB's annual report."

Isaac was not sure whether Ishmael's objective was to fake him out. He had never observed Ishmael looking at the numbers, let alone discussing them. They focused their attention on the operating revenues.

An **annual report** is a yearly record of a company's financial health. The Securities and Exchange Commission (SEC) requires that the report be issued to its shareholders. However, these annual reports should not be confused with the 10Ks required by the SEC, because the annual report published by the company does not have to meet the SEC's disclosure requirements.

"I don't think this is a lot of revenue compared to the big companies, but it shouldn't be compared to big companies. What is important here is the upward trend. If companies are in the business of making money, ACB made some money, mostly through advertising and subscriber fees. They've shown that they have the ability to increase their revenue from year to year. I think that's a good indicator of success. Don't you?" Ishmael asked.

Isaac, still shocked, nodded affirmatively "Just because a com-

---

ANNUAL REPORT - ACB HOLDINGS, INC.

SELECTED CONSOLIDATED FINANCIAL DATA
The following table sets forth, for the periods and as of the dates indicated, selected consolidated financial data for the Company. The selected consolidated financial data for the five years in the period ended July 31, 199-, have been derived from the Company's audited financial statements. This information should be read in conjunction with the Company's consolidated financial statements and notes thereto appearing elsewhere in this annual report.

IN THOUSANDS, EXCEPT PER SHARE AMOUNTS

Year Ended July 31,	1997	1996	1995
Total Operating Revenues	$154,227	$132,275	$115,222

(Includes advertising, subscriber fees, etc.)

---

pany has revenue doesn't mean it's profitable, does it?"

"No," replied Ishmael. "What if the cost of selling the goods or services was more than the revenue generated? What if a company is paying a lot to advertise, but the ads are terrible and no one buys? You have to look beyond the revenue to see if there was any money left over after paying for the cost of doing business. That's the net income." Ishmael felt his confidence growing as he noticed Isaac's attention to his words.

"You see, twin, ACB has been profitable for at least three

> Companies almost never receive money just because they exist. Money enters the company in exchange for products and/or services. This is called income or **revenue**, and is usually the first thing you want to know about a company you are invested in or about to invest in.

IN THOUSANDS, EXCEPT PER SHARE AMOUNTS			
Year Ended July 31,	1997	1996	1995
Net Income	$23,787	$22,063	$19,912

consecutive years. The net income has also increased every year. I like that trend, but I do have some questions you can probably answer," Ishmael began.

Isaac felt his confidence waning. He thought he knew so much more than his brother, then he was reminded of why they were there – to cooperate, not compete. "Well if I don't know the answers, I know where to find them," Isaac said with a smile.

Isaac was beginning to feel comfortable with the thought that he and Ishmael really could learn together and that his lack of knowledge would not be perceived as a weakness, but as an area for growth.

"The difference in total operating expenses between 1995 and 1997 is about 40 %, but the difference in net income is about 20%. Why wouldn't the difference in income be about 40% too? They were making the money," Ishmael asked.

"Brother, you know I haven't followed ACB, but it's probably explained in here somewhere. Let's look." Isaac began flipping through the pages, and they settled on the "Management's Discussion."

MANAGEMENT'S DISCUSSION AND ANALYSIS OF RESULTS OF OPERATIONS AND FINANCIAL CONDITION

RESULTS OF OPERATIONS

ACB Holdings, Inc. (the "Company") operates predominantly in the cable television programming industry. Its cable television programming operations are conducted through Ashanti Cable Broadcasting Network ("ACB")...

LIQUIDITY AND CAPITAL RESOURCES

The Company's principal source of working capital is internally generated cash flow from operations. As reported in its consolidated statements of cash flows, the Company generated net cash from operating activities of $33.5 million during the year ended July 31, 1997. At July 31, 1997, the Company's cash and temporary investments aggregated $7.1 million and *the Company had an excess of current assets over current liabilities of $33.1 million.*

"Whoa!" Isaac shouted, "33 million dollars in cash?!"

Ishmael reminded him that he thought all along that ACB was a good company. "What are the temporary investments mentioned here?" Ishmael did not see anything about temporary investments. He only saw the millions of dollars mentioned.

Isaac confirmed that his brother had good reason to question how the revenue was being used and whether the costs of doing business had increased dramatically. "I don't know how many small companies can state that they have $33.1 million over their debt. Heck, why don't they pay you some of that money for holding their stock? Does ACB pay dividends?"

Isaac and Ishmael flipped throughout the report and found their answer in the Income Statement.

"I guess we really didn't have to look in the report to know that they haven't paid a dividend. I would have known that by looking at my statements. I haven't received extra cash, no

A **dividend** is a distribution of a company's earnings (additional stock, or cash in most cases) to its shareholders. The board of directors determines the amount of payment. If you want your stock investments to generate investment income, buy stocks in companies that have a history of paying dividends.

Year Ended July 31,	1997	1996	1995
Cash dividends Declared	–	–	–

stock, no nothing. Is that reason for me to sell ACB?" Ishmael began to doubt his holdings.

Isaac reassured him that he should not sell ACB just because they did not pay dividends. "What you want to know now is whether the money they could have been paying you is being invested in ways that would potentially increase the value of your stock. What about those temporary investments?" Isaac was eager to return to that question.

They flipped through the pages to find more explanations.

As part of its ongoing strategic plan, the Company plans to continue to invest significant amounts of capital in compatible media and other businesses reaching the Black consumer marketplace. Significant current and potential future fund commitments included a music channel and a coffee shop chain.

"A music channel makes sense to me. It's entertainment, just like shows and movies. But a coffee shop chain?" Ishmael was worried.

"What? Don't Black folks drink coffee?" Isaac chuckled. "Imagine the possibilities – Ashanti Coffee Shop: Coffees from Africa and the Caribbean. I can see it as much as I can smell it. You walk in and immediately you smell Mother Africa. You can order from a variety of countries, and each coffee has it's own taste. Yeah. That could work!" Isaac was often taken by new business ideas without determining whether the company was best suited to exploit the opportunity.

Ishmael could not imagine an entertainment business getting into coffee. "Television to coffee. Hmm." They read on.

During the year ended July 31, 1997, the Company invested *$1 million* in Music Heaven Records, Inc. (MHR) which distributed musical recordings. The Company is committed to loan (MHR) up to $3 million.

"I don't know Music Heaven Records, Inc. Do you?" Isaac looked to Ishmael for guidance.

"No, but I'm going to trust that ACB knows a good buy

when they see it. I'm going to trust that they know how much to invest and how much to lend. Those numbers look small compared to the cash they have on hand, so I'm not worried. What concerns me is how much they plan to invest in coffee. I'll check the news on that one; they will have some formidable competitors."

Isaac asked that Ishmael keep him up-to date, and let him know whether he should consider buying ACBN. His twin assured him that he would. They were flipping through the pages of the annual report to find the Balance Sheet, when suddenly Isaac shouted, "Stop!"

MANAGEMENT'S DISCUSSION AND ANALYSIS OF RESULTS OF OPERATIONS AND FINANCIAL CONDITION

RESULTS OF OPERATIONS
ACB Holdings, Inc. (the "Company") operates predominantly in the cable television programming industry. Its cable television programming operations are conducted through Ashanti Cable Broadcasting Network ("ACB")…

LIQUIDITY AND CAPITAL RESOURCES
The Company's principal source of working capital in internally generated cash flow from operations. As reported in its consolidated statements of cash flows, the Company generated net cash from operating activities of $33.5 million during the year ended July 31, 1997. At July 31, 1997, the Company's cash and temporary investments aggregated $7.1 million and *the Company had an excess of current assets over current liabilities of $33.1 million.*

"Right here, I want to see this again!" Isaac explained, "If you don't look at this carefully, you might get yourself in big trouble no matter what business the company is in. This is where you find out if the company has the ability to pay it's current debts with assets they already have. It's called the current ratio."

Ishmael looked at his twin as if he was a little crazy. "Brother, we already knew that ACB had money."

Isaac looked at his twin long and hard, then his features softened a bit to allow him to say in a cooperative tone, "I would suggest that we do not take their conclusions for granted, but we need to work at the numbers to decide for ourselves whether their conclusions are reasonable."

Isaac had always been more of the numbers guy, and he was willing to help Ishmael overcome his fear of the numbers. They turned the pages, noted some information, and began their analysis.

"What do you think would happen if ACBN decided to borrowed a lot more money that they didn't have to pay off right away while at the same time their cash flow stayed the same or decreased?" Isaac wanted to make sure Ishmael understood what **current ratio** meant.

"I guess that means the current ratio would increase, and I'd be concerned that when the money they borrowed is due, they'd be able to pay it without having to deplete their cash reserve which hasn't grown or has decreased." Ishmael was ready to take it to the next level. "A company can repay debt with cash or with shareholder equity, so you want to make sure there is enough shareholder equity to deal with the debt."

Isaac assured his twin. "We noted here that there is $62,933,000 of long-term debt and $88,418,000 of shareholder's equity. Divide the debt by the shareholder equity and you get about 0.71%. This is something we want to watch carefully over time.

Ishmael had never considered the financials of a company as deeply as Isaac, but was grateful that his twin had. "Thank you, brother. Brother, I want to apologize for my behavior toward you during these last several years. It seems like Dad's death – I don't really know how to put

If your analysis tells you that the **debt-to-equity ratio** is increasing, the cash reserve is dwindling, the ventures are not as profitable, then the company, in borrowing additional funds, may be throwing money away slowly.

it, but I think I wasn't ready to be a man, you know? I think I took my anger at him out on you and I let us down. I'm really sorry about that."

The Twins Weekend was off to a great start. Both Isaac and Ishmael were relieved, for they had engaged in practically nothing but petty fights since their father died. Their lives and lifestyles seemed to offer little in the way of similarities. When they spoke, there was never that "me too" response of their earlier years, that "Why are you doing that? If I were you, I'd…" response that had tired them both. Ishmael's apology was from the heart. His eyes met Isaac's for the first time in years.

Ishmael looked at his identical twin. His haircut, his smooth shave, and his designer casual wear were not as offensive as they once were. It was as if Isaac were transformed from a "Slick

Rick" to a sophisticated renaissance man. "My brother's a sharp, intelligent man. Gloria should consider herself very lucky."

Isaac felt his twin's sorrow, as if Ishmael had reached inside his soul to articulate Isaac's exact thoughts. Just as Isaac was about to return the apology, his cell phone rang. Ishmael asked him not to answer, but Isaac remembered that he was supposed to call Gloria, and that it was probably her calling. Isaac assured Gloria that he was fine, that he and his brother were having a great time, and that he couldn't wait to see her.

Isaac turned to his brother as they continued through the report. Ishmael's short twisted hair, his ever-present five o'clock shadow, and his non-descript t-shirt and jeans were not as embarrassing as once before. "My brother is his own man, confident of who he is and what he thinks. He never was one to walk the path of least resistance. He's a warrior, a brave fighter for the people. What would his neighbors do, what would they think if they didn't have Ishmael to look up to? Isaac's feelings caught him off guard, but he was glad for the moment to feel some brotherly love. "I accept your apology, man. Let's start being men."

"Isaac! Look!" Ishmael cried. "The CEO is going to buy my shares for $48."

Isaac wanted to know what the shares were trading for.

"About $26. Man, I think you'd better buy some ACBN." Isaac wondered whether ACB would make good on their offer, and then read that they had made purchases in the past.

ACB HOLDINGS, INC.

On September 19, 1997, the Company received an offer from Donald Jackson, its majority shareholder, Chairman and Chief Executive Officer, and Crelton Corp., a major shareholder of the Company, to acquire, through a newly formed entity owned by them, all of the Company's outstanding common stock which they do not own, at a per share price of $48. The offer contemplates financing the purchase of such common stock on terms and conditions customary to transactions of a similar nature, which could result in a significant amount of debt funding by the Company or its successor.

CAPITAL STOCK

During the year ended July 31, 1997, the Company repurchased 149,800 shares of its outstanding Class A common stock at an aggregate cost of $4.1 million...

Why would ACB want to repurchase all their shares? He had a hunch, but wanted it confirmed in the report. The brothers flipped through the report to find the Additional Paid-In Capital.

They looked at years 1994 to 1997 to see that there had not been much of an increase in additional paid-in capital.

"What do you make of the **retained earnings**?" Isaac asked Ishmael. Ishmael saw that retained earnings had increased significantly from 1994 to 1997.

Paid-in capital is the money or stock received by the company in exchange for the stock purchased by investors. More specifically, *additional* paid-in capital includes the excess over par value received from the sale or exchange of capital stock.

CONSOLIDATED STATEMENTS OF CHANGES IN SHAREHOLDERS' EQUITY
IN THOUSANDS OF DOLLARS, EXCEPT SHARE DATA

	Retained Earnings	Additional Paid-In Capital
Balance at July 31, 1994	$38,217	$56,232
Purchase of 301,800 Class A Common shares held in Treasury	–	–
Net income for the year	–	19,912
Balance at July 31, 1995	38,217	76,144
Purchase of 1,518,500 Class A Common shares at 1,518,300 Class B common shares held in Treasury	5,280	–
Exercise of 86,900 Class A common Stock options	1,347	–
Income tax benefit from exercise of Common stock options	312	–
Net income for the year	–	22,063
Balance at July 31, 1996	45,156	98,207
Purchase of 149,800 Class A Common shares held in Treasury	–	–
Exercise of 79,800 Class A Common stock options	1,444	–
Issuance of 3,433 Class A common Shares	85	–
Income tax benefit from exercise of common stock options	438	–
Net income for the year	–	23,787
Balance at July 31, 1997	$47,123	$121,994

Years ended July 31, 1997, 1996 and 1995

"I guess ACB is what you'd call a corporate cash cow! Ishmael replied.

"Moo!" They both began mooing like cows as if to say to each other that overall, they liked ACB's financials.

"Brother, I'm impressed," Isaac confessed. He looked at his twin and smiled the same smile they had shared since birth. "If I had only bothered to look at the numbers and not just relied on my instincts, I might have kept my shares."

Retained earnings is another term for undistributed profits.

The twin brothers concluded their business meeting with a pact, that they would begin putting away childish things, like trying to one-up each other, and become the men their father wanted them to be by being resources for each other.

"I'm keeping my stock," Ishmael concluded.

"And I'm buying some ACBN at the open!" Isaac proclaimed.

ACB Year 6 Events

B-Innovation Magazine, January – The first all-black movie cable channel, ACB Movies/GALAXY! 3, a joint venture between ACB Holdings Inc…and ApplauseApplauseMedia Corporation, bows before a nationwide audience in February.

ACBN Jan-Dec, 1997

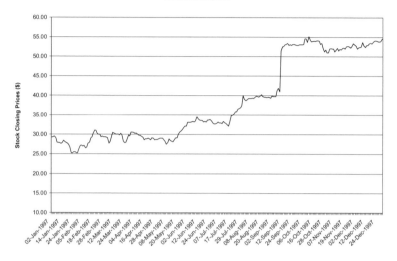

B-Innovation Magazine, May – ACB continues its diversification trend by establishing a new joint venture with Box Clothier to produce an apparel line. "These ventures] are an important part of us leveraging our brand into businesses other than cable television," says Donald Jackson...

B-Innovation Magazine, June – The Street seems to approve of ACB's efforts to increase its hold on the African American market. Some analysts are optimistic about the company's diversification strategy, but other analysts express concern with their moves outside entertainment ....Some say that ACB's low valuation is because of its high free cash flow, that is neither reinvested nor paid out to shareholders in dividends. This is usually a sign of a company's stagnation. The good news is that ACB Holdings has managed to continue growing its core business of cable programming. At press time, it had outperformed the S&P 500 by 6% year to date, and 30% for the past two years. Accordingly, the securities firm Evans & Green considers the stock undervalued and labeled it a buy.

The Street Reports, June 9 – ACB's board authorized opening up to 20 more ACB Coffee Shops over the next five years. Stock rose 12.5 cents to $33.375, reaching a 52-week high. High $33.625, Low $33.25 Close $33.25 Vol 17500

June 12 – ACB reported that fiscal third-quarter earnings jumped 20% as higher revenue from its cable network was somewhat offset by costs associated with new businesses. Net income of $6.3 million, or 36 cents a share for the quarter ended April 30th, up from $5.2 million, or 30 cents a share, a year earlier. Revenue rose 27% to $40.9 million from $32.3 million in the year-earlier period. Price rose $1 to close at $34.50. High $34.50, Low $33.875, Vol 12700.

The D.C. Courier, July – ACB Holdings revenue was $132 million, profit $22 million, earnings per share $1.20, not paying a dividend, shareholder's equity was $66.7 million, return on equity was 33 percent, assets were $150.7 million.

The Street Reports, September 12 – Over the years, ACB has become a cash cow, producing more than $70 million in annual cash flow. The company has only $60 million in debt, but Wall Street hasn't been impressed with how ACB reinvests its cash -- a perception reflected in the stock price. Moreover, the stock has always traded at a discount to its peers, in part because no one believes that Mr. Jackson would sell the company.

September 12 – Jackson made buyback offer, initially for $48 a share. For about 6,020,833 shares amounting to $289 million, $18 more than the high during the last quarter. Price shot up 26%, gaining $10.50 to close at $51.50 *a new high*. Jackson owns 42% of ACB Holdings. ACB reaches 50 million households. COMTELLO, CO. owns 22% of ACB. COMTELLO, CO. loaned Jackson $320,000 and paid $180,000 for 20% of the company. COMTELLO, Co.'s initial loan is worth more than $180 million.

Leslie Bancroft, a shareholder, filed suit in *early September* in Delaware Chancery Court, alleging that the $48 a share offered by Jackson and Crelton Corp., which together owned 90 percent of ACB was too low. Some analysts said ACB was worth as much as $70 a share.

The Street Reports, December 12 – ACB Holdings, Inc. reported a 40% jump in fiscal first-quarter net income due to continuing strength at its Ashanti Cable Broadcasting Network cable network. Jackson told analysts that ACB's basic cable network remained so lucrative that he would have about $300 million in cash, with virtually no debt, to invest in new businesses. For the quarter ended Oct. 31, the Washington State entertainment company said net income was $8.6 million, or 48 cents a share, compared with $6.1 million, or 35 cents a share, year earlier. Revenue rose 18% to $42.3 million from $35.9 million. The previous year's quarter included a charge of $500,000, or three cents a share, tied to a discontinued business. ACB's most recent earnings were well above a First Call consensus of analysts' estimates of 38 cents a share. The company released the results after markets closed.

December 16 – High $53.6875, Low $53.0625 Close $53.250 Vol 18200

December 17 – High $53.625, Low $53.50 Close $53.5 Vol 18600

Year 7

Interdependence is the path to abundance.

Economic Analysis

Ishmael had never visited Isaac at his office. He had to admit that he was impressed with how clean the environment was. It was almost sterile, except for the fact that people from all walks of life were standing in line to talk with a teller or a loan officer or in need of some kind of assistance. It was a far departure from DRC – like night and day. No one was screaming for attention or begging for drugs, money, needles, or assistance. No crowds, just order and quiet. Ishmael thought that if he could have just one day a week where he had order and quiet, he might have time to accomplish something really significant.

As he approached Isaac's office, Ishmael saw his brother's profile. He had a headset on and was gesticulating in a frenzied manner. The door plaque read: "CCAM, Isaac Jamison, Assistant Portfolio Manager." When Isaac noticed Ishmael, he smiled, finished his call and motioned his twin to enter the office. They embraced, and then got down to business.

For the first time in their seven years of investing, they were going to talk about the economy. Their primary concern was whether the Federal Reserve Chairman was going to raise or lower interest rates.

The **Federal Reserve System** (The Fed) was established by the Federal Reserve Act of 1913 for the purpose of regulating the U.S. monetary and banking system. The Federal Reserve System is more commonly referred to as "The Fed." The Fed is comprised of 12 regional Federal Reserve Banks, 24 branches, and other national and state banks. The Fed's main role is to regulate the national money supply.

Isaac was convinced that the prices of stocks, generally, were overpriced, given that there had been a bull market for seven years straight. "The Chairman will have to raise the rates, otherwise people are going to continue paying crazy prices for stocks, and not saving their money or buying bonds."

"So where are the signs of inflation?" Ishmael wanted to know.

Ishmael expected that the Fed would not raise interest rates,

The **Chairman** of the Federal Reserve is the person most listened to with regards to the stock market. Investors want to know what the Chairman is thinking, the reasoning behind his or her thoughts, and what the next decision will be on whether to raise interest rates, by how much and for how long. The Chairman's focus is often on the **rate of inflation**. If inflation is down, there is usually no reason to raise interest rates. If interest rates are not increasing, that is generally a sign to invest in the stock market because the potential for earnings in stocks is greater than bonds, unless of course, interest rates increase dramatically.

"If the cost of credit (in other words, interest rates) still depends on supply and demand. We're in a bull market, because the need for folks to borrow is not all that great. On the other hand, if The Fed needs to tighten the money supply, then okay, I think they will raise rates. But I don't see evidence of it."

Ishmael was proud of himself. He knew that Isaac was blown away that his social-working twin would be able to hold his own in a conversation about economics.

"Twin, what have you been looking at to conclude that The Fed won't raise rates?" Isaac asked.

"The yield curve," Ishmael replied matter-of-factly.

"The yield what?" Isaac replied surprisingly.

"You heard me," Ishmael said, "There's more to making money than investing in stocks. Some folks like bonds, too."

"Isaac, where would you invest your money if you didn't believe you could make money in the stock market?" Ishmael asked.

"I'd first look to see where I could earn the most interest or yield. So, I'd look at bonds first before parking it in cash."

Ishmael confirmed that most reasonable investors would do the same. "But before you sell your stocks to invest in bonds, you'd want to know what the yield curve looks like."

Ishmael explained, "The yield curve is positive but the interest paid on the bonds isn't so

> **Inflation** is a rise in the general level of prices, usually associated with periods of expansion and high levels of employment. When inflation is low, investors tend to feel optimistic or bullish and buy stocks. When there is evidence of inflation, investors tend to feel pessimistic or bearish and sell stocks. The **Consumer Price Index**, referred to as the **CPI**, it is a measure of inflation..

> A **bond** is an interest-bearing security that obligates the issuer (such as a government entity or corporation) to pay the investor a certain rate of interest and the original amount invested at the maturity date. The **yield** (or rate of return) on a bond is calculated using all the interest payments, the purchase price, the redemption (sell) value and the time left until maturity.

To predict the direction of interest rate movements, bond analysts will chart a yield curve. A **yield** curve is a graph plotting the yields of all bonds of the same quality (credit-worthiness) against their maturity periods ranging from the shortest to the longest available. The resulting curve shows if short-term interest rates are higher or lower than long-term rates. If short-term rates are lower, it is called a **positive yield curve**. If short-term rates are higher, it is called a **negative yield curve**. If there is little difference between the two, it is called a **flat yield curve**. The most common version of the curve plots Treasury securities, showing the range of yields from a three-month treasury bill to a 20- or 30-year treasury bond.

attractive that people would prefer them to stocks in the market. It also doesn't appear that yields are going to be that more attractive anytime soon. In order to make them very attractive, the Fed would have to raise rates so high that it would seriously disrupt the stock market.

"Based on consumer sentiment alone, I believe the Fed will raise interest rates," Isaac interjected. "This crazy spending has got to slow down!"

"I cannot believe my brother has become bearish! What!? Are you afraid you've

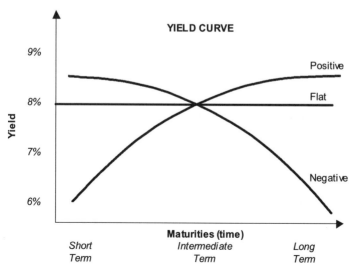

made too much money, and now you're getting a little nervous?" Ishmael teased. "You cannot predict what The Fed will do based on stock prices alone. You have to look at the money." But Isaac had never been one for thorough analysis and deliberated conclusions.

> In order to slow the growth of an economy fueled by the purchase of stocks, The Fed may preemptively raise the **federal funds interest rate** (the rate banks use to lend to each other overnight) and the official discount rate (used rarely when The Fed lends directly to the banks). Stock investors looking for short-term gain usually prefer that The Fed not raise rates, even if it is the right thing to do for the overall economy.

"Well Mr. Treasury, let me ask you this. True or not: are people using their credit cards more than ever? Filing bankruptcy and whatnot? If so, why do you think there is so much money floating around if people are charging stuff?" Isaac was sure that Ishmael could not wiggle out of this corner.

"You work in a bank, right? Then you've probably noticed that the folks who are borrowing money fall into two categories: those who borrow a lot and have sufficient assets for collateral, and those who borrow a lot without assets. Those who borrow the most tend to be people with a high net worth. For better or worse, our people who are up to their necks in debt have the least significant impact on the economy…Thank, God."

Isaac was shocked that his politically progressive twin would say "his people," the ones he has worked for all these years, have an insignificant impact on the economy. However, in the context of their discussion, he realized that Ishmael was being more scientific than usual. And this was not about drug addicts, it was about

Leading Indicators

Economists look at a number of indicators to indicate the health of the economy, starting with the **Gross Domestic Product**. The GDP is a measure of U.S. economic production and spending and includes consumer spending, investments, exports minus imports and government spending. Investors often make buy and sell decisions based on one new piece of information. To get the best understanding of the economy as a whole, look to the Leading Indicators, studies that theoretically show the beginning of an economic trend:

- Average workweek in manufacturing. The National Association of Purchasing Management (NAPM) queries purchasing executives at hundreds of companies. An NAPM reading above 50 might suggest an increase in manufacturing activity. Below 40 may indicate a decrease in activity.
- Average weekly initial claims for state unemployment compensation.
- New orders for consumer goods. If sales are higher than estimated, the stock market usually reacts favorably.
- Deliveries by vendors. A slowdown tends to have a negative impact on the market.
- Contracts and orders for plant and equipment. Increases tend to have a positive impact.
- Building permits (housing starts). If people are buying homes at a faster rate than expected, it is usually good for the stock market.
- Durable Goods Orders. Goods are considered "durable" if they last a long time. If the report is positive, that is usually positive for the stock market.
- Industrial Production. If factories, utilities and mines are producing at a faster pace than estimated, the stock market usually reacts favorably.
- Prices for imported/exported goods. Rising prices of goods are not good if consumers are unable to buy the goods.
- Producer Price Index. Referred to as the PPI, it is an index of commodity prices. If the PPI rises higher than estimated, the stock market usually does not react favorably.
- Consumer Sentiment. A rising confidence in buying is usually positive for the stock market.

For a general indication, look for the Index of Leading Economic Indicators (published by The Conference Board). If the reading is higher than estimated, that's usually an indication that investors will invest more money.

the direction of the economy – who was driving it and who was watching it go by.

"Twin, let me ask you a question. Are we in the beginning of a very, very long bull market, in the middle of a long bull market, or at the peak and about to pull-back?"

Ishmael looked confused for a moment, then thought about the Lagging Indicators.

"Isaac, I really don't think there's a strong indication that we've reached the peak in this business cycle," Ishmael answered.

The Money supply is divided into four categories: M1 – M4. M1 consists of dollars and coins (currency)and **demand deposits** that can be converted to *currency immediately*. M2 includes M1 and some time deposits that are fairly easy to convert into demand deposits. M3 includesM1 and M2, and time deposits of more than $100,000 and **repurchase agreements** with terms longer than one day. M4 includes all of the above, plus long-term liquid assets like **treasury bills**, **savings bonds**, **commercial paper**, bankers' acceptances and Eurodollars.

Isaac was impressed with his twin, and wondered why he had kept his knowledge of the economy a secret from him and their mother.

"Twin, maybe you're right, but just because the scientific analysis doesn't suggest why the Fed might raise interest rates, there might be a compelling reason to prevent inflation."

Ishmael assured Isaac that he was not keeping secrets. After a year dedicated to learning, he was finally beginning to get the big picture. "It's kind of funny, because lately I've even considered the value of the dollar versus the yen. Can you imagine that?"

Lagging Indicators are factors that change after the economy has been in a particular trend, including:

- Average duration of unemployment ;
- Ratio of deflated inventories to sales, manufacturing and trade;
- Labor cost per unit of output (manufacturing);
- Commercial and industrial loans outstanding;
- Corporate profits; and
- Ratio of consumer installment credit to personal income

The Fed can raise and lower rates, and decide the amount by which the change will happen. For example, The Fed can increase rates by a quarter of a point, one-half a point, a point, etc. The greater the increase, the more likely there will be a negative impact on the stock market. The Fed can raise the rates by a quarter of a point and state a "neutral bias" towards raising the rates again soon. If so, the stock market may be positively impacted. An active Federal Reserve Chairman will seek to keep gains in the stock market reasonable.

"I'm not completely surprised given that you minored in history, Ishmael. It makes sense that you'd know something about international issues. So, what's your opinion on the trade deficit – Is the fact that we import more than we export a problem?" Isaac realized he was looking toward Ishmael for guidance.

"If the deficit widens, and foreign currency strengthens against the value of the dollar, the impact on the stock market tends to be negative," Ishmael answered.

"Why is that?" Isaac asked.

"You see, a weaker dollar would raise the price of imports which could cause a rise in inflation that might cause The Fed to raise interest rates," Ishmael concluded with a smile. "Thus, maybe I wasn't considering everything in my analysis and you're right, the Fed might start raising interest rates. Touché, Twin."

"But, Twin, you know what?" Isaac modestly acknowledges his win, "I've been working in this bank for six years now, and I've heard a lot and seen a lot. Do you remember when I worked in the cubicle and complained that I wasn't challenged? Well, I've been an assistant portfolio manager for a couple of years now, and…" Isaac stopped short, looked around the office, and leaned into Ishmael. "I think we can do this ourselves. What would you think about going into the money management business? And before you say why you can't, let me tell you why you can and should."

Isaac began to tell Ishmael what had been on his mind for the last two years. How he had come to appreciate Ishmael's instincts about investing; that few African-Americans invested in large part because they did not understand how; that there were

---

One indication that The Fed might change interest rates is the changing relationship in value between the dollar and the **yen** (currency in Japan). If the yen's value increases, it might spur inflation because Japanese imports (such as cars and electronics) would become more expensive. The value of the dollar is evaluated against the value of the yen because the U.S. is considered the largest creditor and Japan is considered the largest debtor in the world. With the creation of the Eurodollar as tradable currency throughout Europe, economists may also evaluate the dollar against the yen and the Eurodollar.

The **trade deficit** is the difference between the dollar value of U.S. goods and services exported to the rest of the world and the value of goods and services imported into the U.S. from other countries. When the trade deficit widens, and foreign currency strengthens against the value of the dollar, the impact on the stock market tends to be negative because a weaker dollar would raise the price of imports, which could cause a rise in inflation that might cause The Fed to raise interest rates.

few Blacks in the money management business; and that with his trading experience, coupled with Ishmael's instincts and knowledge, they could compete for the investment dollars many of the large firms ignored.

Ishmael sat in the chair facing Isaac and for the first time considered going into business with his brother. As the silence lengthened, Isaac looked nervous, fearing Ishmael would decline the offer Then Ishmael smiled broadly.

"You're on, Twin."

ACB Year 7 Events

January 23 – It was confirmed that Barry Minelli, a New York money manager controlled 1.74 million shares, or 17.3 % of ACB's Class A stock. Minelli bought shares at $48 per share. He was quoted saying, "Forty-eight was too low. Everyone knows that. I'd pay $55."

The Street Reports, March 16 – ACB raises buy back offer to $63 a share, or $378 million for the 32% of the company Jackson did not own.

Chitown Press, March 29 – ACB entered into a partnership with the Fannie Mae Foundation to inform African-Americans about qualifying for a mortgage. ACBN rose $6.06, or 11 percent, to $60.5625.

⌂ *B-Innovation* Magazine, June – Jackson was quoted as saying, "I think the large shareholders I talked to are very pleased with the price... the proposal now goes before the minority shareholders. If a majority of those shareholders approve the $63 buyout proposal, the company will once again be a privately held corporation, held 65% by me and approximately 35% by Crelton Corp."

⌂ *The D.C. Courier*, July 30 – High, ACBN $63, all purchased by Donald Jackson.

Give Me My Money, Please

Some say that everything must change. The truth is that everything changes all the time. Julene could not lose this thought as she sat across the table from her twin sons. It was nearly eight years since her husband's death. And while she missed Marcus' physical presence, she saw that his spirit lived on through Ishmael and Isaac.

> If a company is not operating up to expectations, yet there is a buyer or buyers, the stock price is likely to appreciate.

The twins sat at the dining room table where seven years ago they first discovered their father's brokerage statement. The table was covered with newspapers, magazines, annual reports, 10Ks, brokerage statements, and other documents that Julene did not recognize. Isaac and Ishmael were having an intense discussion, interspersed with laughter and congratulatory pats on the back. They were almost child-like in their conspiratorial giggles. Julene waited for the arguments to begin, but they never did. It looks like my boys have become men, she thought to herself.

"Mom," Isaac interrupted Julene's thoughts, "you won't believe the talks Ishmael and I have had over the last several months. He's taught me stuff about economics, and I've told him some things about trading. And – you won't believe this – we've decided to go into business with each other to help folks invest their money," Isaac announced.

Julene looked at her twins and smiled, not being able to visualize Ishmael as a "financial type" dressed in a pinstriped suit.

"Ishmael, are you ready to leave social services?" Julene asked gently.

Ishmael answered carefully, "I'm ready to help people have more money, and if I can help them do that with a social conscience, then I'm more than ready."

"He's ready, Mom," Isaac chimed in, "and I need him."

Julene asked them when they planned to start. They said they already had commitments for $50,000 from their friends and supporters. She knew it was not enough, and offered them another $50,000.

"Doesn't it take at least $100,000 to get started?" She confirmed two things they had wondered for the last seven years: one, that she knew a lot more about money matters than she let on, and two, that she just wanted to see if they could stop competing, start cooperating, and begin to live the life their father wanted them to live – independently.

"Mom, why didn't you just say that you wanted us to go into business together rather than letting us come to the conclusion seven years after the fact? Don't you think that was a little cruel?" Ishmael cried, "Here I've been, struggling in social services all this time, barely making a living, not having any money to save, let alone invest, and clearly in need of some alternatives. You held back on money that you knew would have helped me, but all the while you were just playing a game. I really don't get it!" Ishmael protested.

Isaac was surprised that his brother, who always said he did not need money, was so upset. He thought later that his anger was not really about the money as much as it was about his mother's manipulation.

Ishmael apologized to his mother for raising his voice. "Mom, I just wouldn't have expected you to do something like that, that's all."

Julene understood why Ishmael was upset. Year after year, she had seen him struggle to make ends meet. She was constantly torn between helping him meet his immediate needs, and trying to help him realize his life's mission.

"It was difficult seeing your struggle, but giving you a few hundred dollars here and there wouldn't have helped you come to this decision. I would have been helping you stay. Plus, I wanted to invest for your benefit. Think about it, seven years ago there was no way you would have been a better investor than B.B., so, had I given the money to you two, I wouldn't have $50,000 to give you now. By the way, the $50,000 is not coming from the principal amount your dad invested; it's from appreciation and dividends. I needed reasons to learn to be a good investor, and you two were my motivation."

Ishmael listened with pride and guilt as their mother explained her rationale. He was so proud that his mother thought so highly of them that she would give them $50,000. Yet, he was ambivalent about taking money that she could use for her needs and wants – a new car to replace the 10-year old one, a roof for the house – to back a risky, new business.

He walked around the table and gave his mother a big hug. She assured him that with her salary, anticipated pension payments, survivor benefits and additional investments through B.B., she could afford to invest in their business. He then walked back to the other side, and reached out his arms to embrace his brother. They reassured each other that they could work well with each other, in time, and that the mission of their business required that they keep learning from each other. The economic welfare of their people was in need of immediate and persistent attention, and they would be the catalyst for improving the financial lives of millions of people.

Ishmael reached for a magazine on the table. "You know what makes me sad? What makes me sad is that a brother can't buy stock in ACB anymore. We could have attracted a lot of folks with ACBN in our portfolio."

"So, you finally made some money, didn't you?" Isaac asked.

"Yes, and so did you." Ishmael replied and began reading the article to his mother and brother...

"Isn't that the most absurd thing you've ever read?!" Ishmael was obviously annoyed. "They had twelve opportunities a year for seven years to write a comprehensive article about ACB, but only after you couldn't invest in it did they think to write about it, calling it a failure because they wanted to branch into other businesses!"

"But Twin," Isaac interjected, "Why would the majority of white folks invest in a Black company only producing shows and products for Black people? And why would you invest in a White-owned company that only offers services and products for White

> *Fortunate* **Magazine** November 9 – "…For most of its publicly traded life, ACBN failed to keep pace either with its peer group of cablecasters let alone the broader market. Wall Street lost interest, and Jackson, eventually concluding that being public hurt, took the company back. What could Wall Street say now? Jackson made his share of mistakes. The Street complains that Jackson squandered cash flow from his highly profitable cable network on pie-in-the-sky, empire-building schemes. Jackson counters that the Street never understood his goal of turning ACB into what he calls "Black America's favorite brand." Not just in media but also in fields as unrelated as restaurants, coffee shops, fashion, and financial services…But Wall Street wants predictable earnings growth, and a logical business plan. Unfortunately Donald Jackson is not predictable, and if his business plan was logical, it was in large part unprofitable outside its core cable network. In retrospect, ACB was fighting an uphill battle from the start…Only about 20% of the stock was ever outstanding, and big chunks of that resided with a few institutions that weren't selling. *The company's Black focus may also have played a role…*

people? Think about it."

The silence was deafening in the room as they thought about the notion of Blacks buying Black, but not investing in Black companies, or not investing at all.

Ishmael looked at the chart and asked, "Do you really think that we – Black business owners and potential owners— believe we are so unworthy of trust from our own people that we will not invest in them?"

"You refused B.B.'s services," Julene offered.

The twins looked at each other with shame, for they knew that deep inside, they doubted his abilities, not really because he talked about cotton, Black history and politics, but because he did not fit the "financial type."

"Our business is in trouble even before it starts!" Isaac feared.

Julene assured them that nothing ventured, nothing gained. "B.B. is retiring next year and looking for someone to take over his client base. Now might be a good time to give him a call, apologize for being disrespectful and rude all these years, and ask him for the opportunity to discuss his succession plans."

Ishmael looked uncomfortable.

"What's wrong?" Julene asked.

"Mr. Freeman wrote me some time ago and asked if Isaac and I would meet with him to discuss our 'life plans'," Ishmael admitted.

Julene confirmed that B.B. was retiring soon.

"And you didn't respond? You haven't given him reason to tell you anything. I'm going to say this one last time. Call B.B."

The Jamison family pondered over the prospects of whether their money management business could also attract members of the Black community before they had to possibly borrow money to buy back their investment, like Donald Jackson. They discussed whether Donald Jackson had read the article in *Fortunate* and if so, whether he regretted ever taking his company public. They wondered whether it was a good move to take it private again, just as African-Americans began investing in greater numbers than before.

They had lots of questions, but only one answer: to provide the information and the services that would allow their people to secure their financial futures. Would it be a grand success? Only time would tell, but the brothers had their initial capital of $100,000, thanks to Mom and Dad. After nearly seven years of social services and bank work, they had garnered the skills and contacts along with social consciousness, fundamental and technical analysis, and enough marketing savvy to pull it off. Ishmael and Isaac, the perfect balance of compassion and capitalism, were two sides of the same coin known as Marcus Jamison. They could clearly see the benefits for themselves, but could they convince an exploited people to *invest in* rather than just *buy from* a once-oppressive economy? That was the question.

The Inheritance

The phone rang in the small Appian Street office.

"B.B. Freeman. Ah, Reverend Jamison's boys?…Uh, huh…Hmmm?…I see…Let's have lunch. I have an opportunity you young men might want to explore." B.B. hung up the phone and returned to his typewriter to continue his correspondence...

...It is with much joy and sadness that I announce my retirement. I'm joyous because over the last 30 years, I expanded Thomas Securities from my little office here to five offices throughout Houston, including downtown. Yes, it's been a wild ride, but I'm ready to pack it up, and leave it to someone who can take it to the next level.

Several years ago I met two young men, twin brothers, whose mother has been my client since her husband passed several years ago. The brothers have the ability to continue Thomas Securities. They are very much like their father was, full of ambition and compassion, but naturally I have concerns about how successful they would be without a dedicated consultant. My greatest concern is their utter confidence and faith in their perception of life. For example, they have no idea that I have 115 brokers working for me, no idea that I prefer working from my first office in what has become the "ghetto", and they have no idea that I am the founder of Thomas Securities. I guess that's youth, but in order for them to make a go of it, they'll need a full-time consultant. There's no way they can manage five offices, so I'll have to consider selling three which would amount to a $4.5 million loss of income for me. I'd better reconsider that.

As I am retiring, I'd like you to find a buyer for the two downtown parking lots. I know you'd like me to keep them because my father left me that land, but I built the lots to generate income, and that I did. That land and Freeman

Parking, are now worth about five million dollars. I know what you're thinking, but my conscious is clear on this one. Thomas Johnston Freeman risked slavery to the land so that his people might have something to justify the Freeman name, and I converted those old plots into modern-day, low cost, income-producing businesses. Looking retirement straight in the face, I've never felt freer. My wife and I are keeping the two lots here as retirement income property. In sum, please find buyers for three of my offices, and two of my lots. Send the contracts to my home, and the checks directly to my bank there. In six months, we'll be your neighbors on the hill.

— The End —

Epilogue

Some offices serve only as places to do business; other offices serve as testaments of faith. One look at the symbols of business success adorning the walls or the scrapbook of magazine articles on the glass coffee table, and you knew you were inside a monument. Looking across the office, you knew you were about to make a quantum leap through history before reaching the desk. Then you began to remember all that had been said about the man.

The office was known throughout the "Black world" to be occupied by one of the most successful Black businessmen in the world. He had been written about in many business magazines, as well as entertainment and gossip publications. You felt like you were in a king's domain, and depending on your allegiances, you were.

The bookshelves held books on subjects from sports to food to fashion, music, motion pictures, finance – you name it. Practically every service, product, institution, fad an African-American would be interested in, was represented in this personal library of business ideas and inspiration.

If you were ever honored enough to sit in the chair facing the desk, you knew you were facing a man that knew how to make alliances and make deals. Yes, it was quite intimidating.

The first founder, president and CEO of a Black company traded on the New York Stock exchange, headed directly for his desk. He began idly reading the latest *Fortunate* magazine, but this time, something caused an emotional reaction:

Fortunate **Magazine** November 9 – "…For most of its publicly traded life, ACBN failed to keep pace either with its peer group of cablecasters let alone the broader market. Wall Street lost interest, and Jackson, eventually concluding that being public hurt, took the company back. What could Wall Street say now? Jackson made his share of mistakes. The Street complains that Jackson squandered cash flow from his highly profitable cable network on pie-in-the-sky, empire-building schemes. Jackson counters that the Street never understood his goal of turning ACB into what he calls "Black America's favorite brand." Not just in media but also in fields as unrelated as restaurants, coffee shops, fashion, and financial services…But Wall Street wants predictable earnings growth, and a logical business plan. Unfortunately Donald Jackson is not predictable, and if his business plan was logical, it was in large part unprofitable outside its core cable network. In retrospect, ACB was fighting an uphill battle from the start…Only about 20% of the stock was ever outstanding, and big chunks of that resided with a few institutions that weren't selling. *The company's Black focus may also have played a role…*

Jackson wondered why *Fortunate* waited until after he took ACB Holdings, Inc, private to write about his company. He began to look through his scrapbook of articles and realized that the publications only took an interest in his public company when there was a crisis: on the day it went public, on the day there were discrepancies about the number of subscribers, and on the day when he announced he would buy back the shares. By and large, there was no sustained interest. Jackson wondered whether the so-called mainstream press was the reason why he had so few investors and why so few African-Americans invested or even knew they could invest in his company. He did not blame anyone, he just wondered.

And he wondered whether his entrée to Wall Street was only historic for himself and his company. He had dreamt of a world where Black people would be more supportive of his efforts, and he in turn could invest in the enterprises of other Black business-men and women. What Jackson knew, Wall Street didn't under-stand, or if they did understand, they didn't agree with the strat-egy, or if they understood and agreed that that strategy was good, they didn't believe Jackson could carry it off. Whatever the rea-sons, Jackson blamed no one.

Jackson picked up his phone book, and turned to the Fs.

"B.B., this is Donald, how are you?...Look, I've given a lot of thought to what you've been telling me these last few years, and I think you were right … Oh, and B.B., I do appreciate your help. Really, I do."

Jackson returned to his book of articles, starting in October, eight years ago…

The Street Reports, October 31 – ACB Holdings, Inc.'s public stock offering, its first, was a hit. The 4.25 million-share offering, 21% of the 11-year-old company, was the Big Board's fourth most active issue. Its underwriters – First Maine Corporation – initially priced the shares at $11 to $13 each, based on price-to-earnings ratios of other cable-TV stocks. The shares began trading under the ticker symbol ACBN at $17 each and closed at $23½. That gives ACB Holdings a market value of about $475 million.....

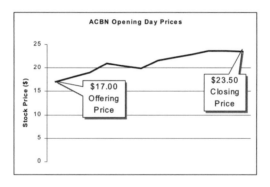

He had no regrets, only plans for the opportunities ahead.

Glossary

One of the most frustrating obstacles to understanding the stock market is the financial jargon. This glossary contains words and phrases that are commonly used. To broaden your financial vocabulary beyond this list, buy and use a financial dictionary.

A

Acquisition. The control of one corporation by another.

Allocation. This is the amount of stock an IPO underwriter will grant an investor. The allocations can vary significantly depending on the indication of interest.

Aggressive Growth Portfolio. A portfolio characterized by high turnover (buying and selling) of stock holdings attempting to cash in on situations involving higher risk and rapid appreciation.

Appreciation. The current value of the investment less the price paid, plus dividends (if any).

Ask Price. The lowest price at which anyone will sell a security at a given time.

Asset. Property owned by an individual, partnership or corporation.

B

Banker's Acceptance. A financing source used often in international trade.

Bear Market. A market in which stock prices are falling.

Bid Price. The highest price anyone will pay for a security at a given time.

Big Board. The slang term for the New York Stock Exchange.

Blue Chip. A well regarded company with a long record of profitable growth, a consistent dividend payment history and a reputation for quality management.

Bond. An interest-bearing corporate or governmental security. It obligates the corporate or governmental issuer to pay the bondholder (investor) a specific amount of money (interest) and repay the principal amount (debt) lent to the issuers at a specific time.

Broker. A person paid a fee or commission for acting as an agent in the buying and selling of securities.

Broker/Dealer. A person or a firm that operates at different times as both a broker and a dealer.

Bull Market. A market in which stock prices are rising.

C

Capital Gain. The profit from the sale of a capital asset.

Capitalization. The total market value of all the outstanding shares of a company's stock. At the time of writing, , companies that are described as "large-cap" have a market cap over $5 billion; "mid-caps" range from $1 billion to $5 billion; "small-caps" from $250 million to about $1 billion; and "micro-caps" are $250 million or less.

Capital Stock. The dollar amount of outstanding shares at the time they were issued and sold, plus the paid-in capital minus any adjustments.

Class A. Common stock that is "classified" or separated from other classes of common stock. Class A shares usually allows the shareholder greater voting power, but one must read the corporation's charter and bylaws to obtain an actual description.

Commercial Paper. Short term (2 to 270 days) debt securities issued by banks and corporations for investors who are not using their cash.

Commission. A fee paid to an agent, advisor or broker for services performed.

Common Stock. Securities representing ownership in a corporation.

Conservative Growth Portfolio. A portfolio with low turnover (low selling), which is likely to contain a higher percentage of "blue chip" securities.

Corporation. An organization chartered by a state government. Most commonly used to describe a business conducted for profit however, there are non-profit corporations and municipal corporations.

Correction. Reverse movement, usually downward, in the price of an individual stock or stock index.

Cost Basis. That portion of an investment not subject to taxation because it was purchased with after tax dollars.

Currency. A medium of exchange.

Current Ratio. Current assets divided by current debts. If a company's cash flow is unpredictable, look for a high current ratio for confidence that the company can pay its liabilities with assets already on hand.

Current Yield. The annual return on an investment expressed as a percentage of the actual amount invested. For stocks, the current yield is the annualized dividend (if any) divided by the current market price of the stock.

Cyclical Stocks. Stocks whose prices tend to rise and fall according to the strength or weakness of the economy, such as automobile companies.

D

Dealer. A person engaged in the trading of securities or commodities for his or her own account and not as an agent for another.

Debt-to-Equity Ratio. Total debts divided by shareholder equity. This should show whether the owner's equity could buffer the creditor's claims if the company runs out of cash, closes it doors, or goes into bankruptcy.

Demand Deposit. The account balance at the financial institution (i.e. bank, credit union) that can be withdrawn without prior notice.

Discount Rate. Interest rate the Federal Reserve charges its member banks for loans.

Dividend. The distribution of cash, stock, or products by a company to its shareholders.

Dollar Cost Averaging. The systematic buying of securities with a fixed number of dollars being committed to each purchase at or around the same time each month. The system is designed to purchase a given dollar value of securities rather than a given number of shares to lessen the average cost of shares.

Due Diligence. This is part of the process of taking a company public. Investment bankers and lawyers for the underwriters conduct an in-depth examination of the proposed IPO by speaking with the company's management team about the company's prospectus, business strategy, competitors and financial statements.

E

EDGAR. Established by the Securities and Exchange Commission (SEC), this is the system used by companies and mutual funds to file documents electronically.

Eurodollar. United States currency held in banks outside the U.S. used for settling international transactions.

Equity. The interest of shareholders in a company.

Equity Market. A market in which stocks are sold.

Equity Security. Any stock or similar security which gives the shareholder an interest in the earnings and assets of the issuer.

F

Federal Reserve Board (FRB). Seven people appointed by the President of the U.S. to 14-year terms to establish policies for the Federal Reserve System including setting the discount rate, credit availability, and margin requirements. Also known as the "Fed."

First Day Close. The closing price at the end of the first day of trading of newly issued stock. The first day close theoretically reflects not only how well the leading underwriting manager priced and placed the stock, but what the near-term trading is likely to be. For example, IPOs that shoot up 100 percent or 200 percent on their first day of trading are likely to fall back in price on subsequent days as a result of profit taking.

Fundamental Analysis. The study of the basic factors underlying stock price performance relative to the corporation's product and service sales and profitability trends.

G

Growth Stock. Shares of a corporation that is expected to show above-average gains in profitability and share price appreciation.

H

Holding Company. A company that holds a controlling financial interest in another company.

I

Income Portfolio. Investment concentrated on corporations with records of consistently high dividend payments or on high quality bonds.

Index. A group of stocks that represent a segment of the stock market. For instance, the Dow Jones Industrial Average ("DJIA" or "Dow") is an index of thirty large, publicly traded U.S. companies. The Standard & Poors' 500 ("S&P 500") is an index of the 500 largest publicly traded U.S. companies.

Initial Public Offering. Also known as an IPO, the first time a corporation sells stock to the public.

Insider. Someone who is a director, officer or principal shareholder. Their position with respect to the management of the company allows them greater access to information before the general public. In order to ensure confidence in the stock market, insiders are restricted in trading securities based on information not possessed by the general investing public.

Investment Adviser. The company employed by a mutual fund to advise it in the investment, supervision, and management of the assets of the mutual fund.

Investment Advisory Service. People who are registered with the SEC and provide investment advice and/or money management for a fee.

Investment Banker. An agent or underwriter that serves as the middleman between the investing public and the issuer of the securities (the company or government).

Investment Company. Companies principally engaged in the business of investing the funds of its shareholders. Such companies are almost always registered with the Securities and Exchange Commission under the regulations of the Investment Company Act of 1940.

Investment Company Act of 1940. Legislation that requires investment companies to register with the SEC and abide by standards in security pricing, promotions, and other areas of investment company operations.

L

Liability. The legal responsibility to repay debt.

Liquidation. The process of terminating and closing down a business.

Lock-Up Period. The lead underwriter restricts insiders from selling their shares for a period of time. However, the lead underwriter has the option of lifting the lock-up period earlier. Knowledgeable investors track the termination of lock-up periods, knowing that stocks may weaken in price around that time.

Long. Being "long" in a security means that you own it.

M

Majority Shareholders. The combined shares of one or a variety of shareholders amounts to more than 50% of the shares.

Margin. Used to describe a purchase of an investment through borrowing from the trader or broker.

Margin Call. A demand by a broker than an investor deposit additional collateral (securities, cash, etc.) against borrowed funds.

Market Value. The price at which a security sells in the marketplace.

Merger. The combination of two or more companies.

Minority Shareholders. The combined shares of a variety of shareholders amounts to less than 50% of the shares outstanding.

Money Market. A market in which short-term debt obligations are traded. Also used to refer to the actual cash or short-term debt obligations that are much like cash.

Mutual Fund. An investment company that pools the money of many investors with the benefit of investing more effectively than the individual alone. The fund manager is responsible for choosing a combination of stocks, bonds and cash.

N

NASDAQ. The National Association of Securities Dealers Automated Quotation System is a computerized system that provides brokers and dealers with price quotations for securities traded over-the-counter. The (NASDAQ) system keeps track of the quotations of the most frequently traded over-the-counter stocks.

O

Offering Price. This is the price at which the IPO is first sold to the public. The lead underwriting manager sets it, usually after the close of stock market trading the night before the shares are distributed to IPO buyers

Option. Generally speaking, it is a contract to buy or sell securities for a specified sum. If the right to buy or sell is not acted upon (exercised), the right to do so expires and the purchaser of the contract forfeits the money paid for the contract. An option can also be an agreement tied to an index. There are call options that gives the buyer the right to buy shares of an underlying security at a fixed price before a specified date. There are also put options, which gives the buyer the right to sell shares within a specified period of time.

Outstanding. Stock that is held by shareholders.

Over-the-Counter (OTC). A network of broker-dealers who trade securities over the phone rather than through an exchange.

P

Par Value. The price assigned a share for purposes of completing the company's balance sheet. There is no real relationship between the par value and the market value.

Point. The unit of measure of securities prices, one point = 1 percentage point or about $1. For example, if a stock is "up a point," its price has risen by about $1.

Portfolio. The total investments of an individual or investment company.

Preferred Stock. Stock possessing a priority claim over common stock as to both dividends and distributions in liquidation.

Price-to-Earnings Ratio. The price of a stock divided by its earnings per share.

Prime Rate. The interest rate major banks charge their best business customers.

Principal. The amount of money borrowed, financed, or invested. Also, a dealer who buys and sells for his or her own account, or an individual for whom a broker executes an order.

Prospectus. The official circular that describes the securities being offered for sale. It must include material information, but not all information.

Public Offering. Securities made available to the public in general, not just a limited group of individuals.

Public Offering Price. The price at which securities are offered to the public.

Q

Quiet Period. After the IPO is priced, the underwriters generally face further restrictions on issuing research.. It usually lasts up to 25 days. However, under some special circumstances the underwriters can issue a research recommendation more quickly.

R

Rally. A rise in the market or an individual stock, following a general decline in price levels.

Repurchase Agreement. Also referred to as "repos," these are agreements between traders that the seller will repurchase the security sold at an agreed upon price and an agreed upon time.

Risk. The possibility of negative returns. Investments with a low-risk profile are generally classified as "conservative," while those with a high-risk profile are generally classified as "aggressive."

S

Savings Bonds. Government-issued securities that mature in 10 years, ranging in denominations from $50 to $10,000. Taxpayers saving for their children's college education may collect interest without federal taxation (Please consult your tax preparer or accountant for more information).

Securities and Exchange Commission (SEC). The federal regulatory agency created by the 1934 Securities Exchange Act to enforce federal securities laws and regulations.

Security. According to the Securities Act of 1933, the evidence of an investment in an enterprise with the expectation that a profit will be made from the efforts of others. Sector. A group of stocks that belong to related industries or share some other characteristic, e.g. international, small-cap, etc.

Shares. Also referred to as "stocks," these are ownership interests in a company.

Shareholder. Someone who owns stock in a corporation.

Short Sale. The sale of securities not owned with the expectation that the same securities can be purchased at a lower price in the near future.

Spread. The difference between the bid price and the asked price. The purchase of one security, option or contract against the sale of another with the expectation that the "spread," or price difference, will provide for a profit.

Stock. Ownership interest in a company.

Stock Exchange. A location where brokers and dealers meet to execute orders placed by institutions and individuals to buy and sell stocks (and bonds and other securities).

T

Technical Analysis. The study of stock price patterns in an effort to anticipate future moves.

Time Deposits. A certificate of deposit (CD) or a savings account held in a bank or other financial institution for a term or can only be withdrawn with prior notice.

Total Return. The capital appreciation of an investment, plus all dividends and interest received.

Treasury Bill. A short-term (matures within a year) government security that is discounted and sold at auctions in denominations from $10,000 to $1,000,000.

U

Underwriter. An investment banker or group of investment bankers who agree to purchase a new issue of stock from the issuing company, and distribute it to investors. If an underwriting group forms, they create a temporary organization for the purpose of selling the stock. The underwriters enter into an "agreement among underwriters" to purchase the stock and sell them at an agreed upon price and then to resell them at a public offering price.

V

Valuation. See Price-to-Earnings Ratio.

Y

Yield. The income return on an investment, calculated as a percentage of the price. Yields change in the opposite direction from prices.

15 Simple Lessons

for Stock Investors

LESSON ONE: Do not act on unfounded expectations.
Conjecture and expectations about what people will or will not invest in the future is based merely on the current stock price. Do not sell stock on unfounded expectations alone.

LESSON TWO: Do not refuse to sell just because you have an emotional attachment to an investment.
Don't make assumptions about the quality of an investment based on "warm and fuzzy" feelings . Your investment will appreciate, depreciate or both at varying periods of time. Do the homework to provide good reasons for keeping your stock.

LESSON THREE: Do not invest without adequate understanding.
If you do not want to wait until you understand *everything* about investing before getting started, consult with a professional. However, even after you entrust your investments to a professional, seek to understand what you are invested in and why.

LESSON FOUR: Know your financial objectives before you buy or sell stock.
Everyone has different financial priorities. Just because one person owns a particular stock doesn't mean you should too. Ask yourself the question, "What would I like my net worth to be in 5, 10, 25 and 50 years?" If owning the stock does not have the potential to appreciate in price enough to help you reach those quantified goals in the set period of time, you should not own it.

LESSON FIVE: Know the company best able and willing to capitalize on the exploitable business opportunity.
What other companies compete with the company you are considering? What is the company's market share? What is happening in their market-

place, with their customers and potential customers? Are there any major threats to the company's success, such as a competitors, regulations, new technology? Put your investment options in context with the rest of the world. If the company you choose cannot grow and expand, neither will your investment.

LESSON SIX: Diversify your investments across companies and industries.
It's okay to spread your investments across several companies, but how diverse is your portfolio by industry. For example, if you invest only in companies in the high technology industry, you risk any change in perceptions. If the investing public feels pessimistic about high tech, companies in that industry may suffer. On the other hand, if the high technology industry is perceived as being the industry with the most growth potential, the reward potential is high.

LESSON SEVEN: Create your own strategy for diversifying your stock portfolio.
There are two overall strategies for creating a diversified portfolio – top-down or bottom-up.
1) The top-down strategy is when the investor first looks at trends in the general economy, and then selects industries, and then companies that should benefit from those trends.
2) The bottom-up strategy is when the investor looks at the performance of the company first. The belief is that no matter the state of the economy, these companies will perform well.

LESSON EIGHT: Know the industry groups.
The industry groups include: Basic & Raw Materials, Capital Goods, Conglomerates, Consumer Cyclicals, Consumer Non-Cyclicals, Energy, Financial, Healthcare, Industrial, Technology, Telecommunications, Transportation, and Utilities. Certain industries tend to experience more growth or more stagnation or loss depending on the current economic cycle. Consequently, you will have a greater chance of investing successfully if you know the industry groups poised to do well in the present economic cycle.

LESSON NINE: Determine what professional analysts say about your stocks or the stocks you're interested in buying.
An analyst works with a brokerage house, bank, or mutual fund, and studies the business practices, products, financials and markets of companies. They then make recommendations on whether investors should buy, sell, or hold stock. The *Wall Street Journal* and Institutional Investor rank analysts by the accuracy of their estimates.

LESSON TEN: Invest with as much information as you can gather and understand.
You take more risk than necessary by investing without information. Treat your investment dollars as if that money belonged to a loved one. Ask questions and seek out information.

LESSON ELEVEN: Determine your objective: to be a stock trader or a better investor.

LESSON TWELVE: Invest with changing market conditions in mind.
If your stocks are not meeting your expectations and do not have the potential to meet your expectations in the time frame you have set for reaching your goals, re-evaluate not only the fundamental trends, but your tolerance for risk. It may be that holding onto the stock is inconsistent with your growth, income or growth and income objective.

LESSON THIRTEEN: Mutual funds may provide an appropriate alternative to a self-directed and excessively traded stock portfolio.
Excessive trading on a variety of stocks can be confusing. If you want your investment dollars spread across companies and industries, and you either do not have enough money to spread around, or you have the money, but not the time, consider mutual funds. Mutual funds are invest-

ment companies whereby the investments are chosen and managed by the fund manager or team of managers. It is typical for a mutual fund to own tens of stocks and trade often.

LESSON FOURTEEN: Focus not only on price trends, but volume trends too.
You may be able to identify a change in the perception of the stock before the price changes.

LESSON FIFTEEN: Do not let an index alone dictate your investment objectives.
The NASDAQ Composite Index was especially noteworthy and newsworthy in 1999 because it closed the year up 85.6%. No other index in the history of indexing stocks had such an increase in one year. The dramatic increase was difficult to ignore. But in the year 2000 it began slipping downward.

About the Author

Pamela Ayo Yetunde, a financial consultant with a New York investment firm, works with individuals, small business owners, and not-for-profit organizations. With degrees in journalism and law, she has worked as a journalist in The Netherlands, a political organizer, and a human rights advocate.

Her first book, *Beyond 40 Acres and Another Pair of Shoes: For Smart Sisters Who Think Too Much, and Do Too Little Around Their Money Matters* broke ground in addressing money topics from social, cultural, political and psychological perspectives.

A native of Indianapolis, Indiana, Ms. Yetunde currently resides in California and can be reached at pay@smartsisters.com.

For additional copies of this book, please send check or money order for $15 (plus S&H&T of $3.50) to:

Marabella Books
4096 Piedmont Avenue PMB 307
Oakland, CA 94611
(510) 337-3262

http://www.smartsisters.com